Godparenting

Godparenting

Nurturing the Next Generation

NANCY ANN MCLAUGHLIN

and

TRACEY E. HERZER

Church Publishing
NEW YORK

Church Publishing
19 East 34th Street
New York, NY 10016
www.churchpublishing.org

Cover art: Dianne Robbins

Cover design: Laurie Klein Westhafer

Library of Congress Cataloging-in-Publication Data

Godparenting : nurturing the next generation / Nancy Ann McLaughlin and Tracey E. Herzer.
    p. cm.
ISBN-13: 978-0-8192-2267-1 (hardcover)
ISBN-13: 978-1-64065-035-0 (paperback)
1. Sponsors. 2. Parenting—Religious aspects—Christianity. I. Herzer, Tracey E. II. Title.
BV1478.M35 2007
248.8'45—dc22

                            2007023785

Printed in the United States of America

Contents

Introduction   vii

Chapter 1:
   "Me? A Godparent?" Awakening to a New Role   1

Chapter 2:
   "I'd Like You to Meet Someone Special": Getting to
      Know God   17

Chapter 3:
   "What's for Supper?" Formation, Fellowship, Bread,
      and Prayers   36

Chapter 4:
   "Gotta Get Washed Up": Whenever You Fall . . .   57

Chapter 5:
   "Once upon a Time": Sharing God's Story with
      Your Godchild   76

Chapter 6:
   "Ouch! I'll Bet That Hurt!" Loving Your Neighbor   91

Chapter 7:
   "That's Not Fair!" God's Justice and Peace   112

Chapter 8:
   "I Can Do It Myself!" Renewing the Covenant Made
      at Baptism   130

Introduction

We wrote this book for godparents of all kinds: the official ones who stand up as baptismal sponsors in church, but also for the "unofficial godparents" in our lives—parents, teachers, mentors, coaches, friends—anyone who is looking for real and significant ways to help foster spiritual development in a child they care about. In the service of Holy Baptism, the whole church family is called to help encourage and sustain this new Christian. The entire congregation promises to support not only the newly baptized person, but the parents and godparents as well: "Will you who witness these vows do all in your power to support these persons in their life in Christ?" And we respond with a resounding, "We will" (Book of Common Prayer, 303).

The purpose of this book is to introduce godparenting as one of the most special relationships two Christians can share. It will offer some historical background of this important role, and also offer practical suggestions for discussions or activities to share with your godchild.

This book is organized around phrases from the service for Holy Baptism, found on pages 299–311 in the Episcopal

Book of Common Prayer. Chapter 1 uses the first question asked of the parents and godparents, "Will you be responsible for seeing that the child you present is brought up in the Christian faith and life?" Chapters 2–7 are based on the questions of our baptismal covenant. Each chapter contains background information, Scripture readings, and various activities that can be used in home or church settings. Chapter 8 concludes the book, using words from the prayers for the baptismal candidates, and helps us look forward to the day when your godchild will renew his or her baptismal covenant in daily confirmation of the faith that has been passed on to a new generation.

You may notice that the pronouns used for your godchild alternate from chapter to chapter: feminine in the first chapter, masculine in the second, and so on. This is an attempt to achieve gender neutrality without resorting to the cumbersome "his/her" or "he/she" throughout.

Because the network of available tools is ever expanding, we also invite you to visit our website *www.god parenting.info* for additional materials. There you will find reading lists and other suggestions for supplemental resources as well as information for church groups, such as available trainings and speakers.

We hope the collected wisdom in this book will help you fully embrace the sacred role of godparent and will serve as a springboard for your own creative adaptations. The ideas in this book are a place to begin thinking about your role as godparent, but as in many relationships, there is much that cannot be taught, but rather must be experienced as God's Spirit leads. We encourage you to open your heart and your imagination and see what happens as you live into this unique and ongoing relationship. As you journey, we pray that the relationship between you and your godchild will grow—sometimes with the godparent leading the way, sometimes with the child running ahead, but hopefully most often as a joint experience where two Christians can go forth together hand-in-hand and explore the world God has made.

Chapter 1

"Me? A Godparent?"

Awakening to a New Role

"Will you be responsible for seeing that the child you present is brought up in the Christian faith and life?"

Ding! A bell rings to wake you up and call you into a new day. Ding! A bell rings to tell you it is time to change classes, change direction, try something new. Ding! A bell rings to remind you of an appointment, a responsibility you have, a place you need to be. Ding! A bell rings to call your attention to someone who needs you at your door.

Ding! You're a godparent!

The sound of a bell has always been meaningful—it can signal danger, induce alertness, or call people together. Bells ring from a church steeple to begin a service, to mark a somber occasion, or to happily herald a celebration of great joy. In Tibet, Buddhist monks use a "bell of mindfulness" as a reminder: When they hear the tone of the bell, it reminds them to listen carefully for the voice of their Creator breaking into their everyday life. The sound of the bell calls them back to their contemplative center and reminds them of who they truly are.

Being asked to become a godparent is a bit like hearing a bell. It can awaken you to a new role and move you in a new direction. It reminds you of your responsibility, and it calls your attention to someone who needs you. Godparents have the opportunity to play a unique role in the life of a child, even for children who are lucky enough to have lots of adults who care for them. Today many children have multilayered, complicated social networks that could include biological parents, adoptive parents, stepparents, foster parents, or grandparents. In addition, children may have other adults who nurture them, such as teachers, coaches, Sunday school teachers, cub scout leaders, and more. So with all these adults around, you might be tempted to wonder, "What is the point of having *godparents* at all?"

At its most basic definition, a godparent is someone who is willing to share the Christian life with another person and help with her religious formation. Ideally parents will be the primary godparents (see BCP, 298: "It is fitting that parents be included among the godparents of their own children"), but other godparents can support the parents and expand the ways that a child experiences God. Parents carefully choose a few official godparents to stand as sponsors for the child during the rite of baptism. The godparents present the godchild as a candidate for Holy Baptism and "thereby signify their endorsement of the candidates and their intention to support them by prayer and example in their Christian life" (BCP, 298).

Being asked to serve as an official godparent in a child's baptism is a distinct honor, and this book will talk about that role in great detail. However, there are also many "unofficial godparents"—adults who have accepted the sacred responsibility to act as a Christian mentor and guide to someone else. Whether your godparent status is official or unofficial, being a godparent is important work, but it does not have to be intimidating. This new role does not mean you are a biblical scholar or that you have worked out all the answers in your own faith journey. It simply means you are willing to walk part of the ancient Way with your godchild, sharing some of what you have learned, as you continue looking together for the next steps on your path.

Renee's Story: True Godparents

The church where I grew up didn't have "official" godparents, but an older couple there were probably the closest thing to godparents you could have without actually calling them that. Their names are Fred and Norma and I named multiple stuffed animals after Norma. When my brother was born, I stayed with them for a week so my mom could settle in without having to worry about me. Any time my parents were on vacation, we stayed with this couple. When I was in high school, they moved away to be closer to their kids, but when I was in college and my choir had a tour stop in their town, they came to hear the concert, and it was just the best thing ever to have someone in the audience who had known and loved me my whole life. They were at my wedding last fall and the first thing Norma said to me at the reception was "cheese cottage." I burst out laughing. One of my favorite books as a child had been about a mouse who lived in Cheese Cottage, and I made them read that book to me probably about a million times. For Norma to remember that was just delightful! It brought back so many memories of how they cared for me.

As a godparent, you can contribute to a child's spiritual development and help her cultivate her own unique relationship with God. You can also help your godchild make connections with other people who reflect God's love and help her learn more about the God who loves us all. Godparents have the wondrous task of helping a child learn to see that she is a beloved child of God—a literal God-child. The most amazing thing about this new relationship, however, is that not only will your godchild benefit from your instructions and example, but *you* will benefit from the ways in which this child can enrich and deepen your own Christian experience. The godparent/godchild relationship is a two-way street between two children of God. We see this reflected in the word origins for "godparent," one of which was the Anglo Saxon "*god sib*"—a term used in the Middle Ages to describe the sponsor as a relative or "sibling" in God's family.

The History of Godparents—Part 1: The Tradition of Sponsors

Although the role of godparents (also called sponsors) has changed and developed over time, the core responsibilities of helping someone encounter and be transformed by God is something we see even in ancient biblical stories:

> When Jesus returned to Capernaum after some days, it was reported that he was at home. So many gathered around

that there was no longer room for them, not even in front of the door; and he was speaking the word to them. Then some people came, bringing to him a paralyzed man, carried by four of them. And when they could not bring him to Jesus because of the crowd, they removed the roof above him; and after having dug through it, they let down the mat on which the paralytic lay. When Jesus saw their faith, he said to the paralytic, "Son, your sins are forgiven." (Mark 2:1–5)

Perhaps the people in this story are not ones you would classify as modern godparents, but they are a wonderful example of the original type of sponsors—people who brought their loved one directly to Jesus. The dedicated friends in this story are "sponsors" in every sense of the word. They went to great lengths and used extraordinary means to accomplish their task, believing completely that if they could just get their friend to Jesus, healing would follow. Can you think of other Bible stories where people brought someone to Jesus?

What Does Baptismal Liturgy Mean?

The word "liturgy" is most often translated as "the work of the people" and is usually used to describe the particular order of a specific worship service. Episcopalians speak of the "liturgy of baptism" or having a "liturgical service," which means there are defined and deeply symbolic elements

God's Words about Baptism

Baptism of Jesus	Matthew 3:13–17
Baptism with Spirit on Pentecost	Acts 1:12–14; 2:1–4
Holy Spirit's importance	Acts 8:9–17
Three thousand people are baptized	Acts 2:1–47
Water as key element	Acts 8:36–40
Families baptized together	Acts 16:13–34
One body and one Spirit	Ephesians 4:4–6
Symbol of death, burial, and resurrection	Romans 6:3–5

and ways to be actively involved in the baptism ceremony that help underscore the meaning of this sacred ritual.

The first Book of Common Prayer, written in 1549, gives specific instructions for the baptism liturgy. It starts with the priest meeting "the Godfathers, Godmothers, and people, with the children" at the church door. After the Lord's Prayer and creed, the priest is instructed to "take one of the children by the right hand, the others being brought after him" as they enter the church, walk through the congregation, and approach the baptismal font. Here the priest addresses the godparents:

Well beloved friends, you have brought these children here to be Baptized, you have prayed that our Lord Jesus Christ would vouchsafe to receive them, to lay his hands upon them, to bless them, to release them of their sins, to give them the kingdom of heaven, and everlasting life. You have heard also that our Lord Jesus Christ has promised in his gospel, to grant all these things that you have prayed for: which promise he for his part, will most surely keep and perform. Wherefore, after this promise made by Christ, these infants must also faithfully for their part promise by you, that be their sureties, that they will forsake the devil and all his works, and constantly believe God's holy word, and obediently keep his commandments. (BCP (1549), "Public Baptism")

The liturgy of baptism uses many symbols. The main symbol, of course, is the water that reminds us how the Spirit of God hovered over the face of the waters before Creation, how the Israelites were led through the Red Sea waters into the land of promise, and how Jesus was baptized in the waters of the Jordan River. But there are other symbols as well: The forehead of the newly baptized person is marked with oil—a symbol of God's Spirit. The baptized person is often dressed in white—a symbol of purity and new life. She is often given a candle—a symbol of God's presence. As you prepare for this important liturgy, take careful notice of all the symbols.

Getting Ready for the Baptismal Liturgy

≷ Find the service of Holy Baptism in the Book of Common Prayer, pages 298–314. Read through the entire service.

≷ Notice the roles of godparents. What are you being asked to say and do? What things come to mind as you read these vows?

≷ Read the additional directions (pp. 312–13) to discover optional roles for godparents (or sponsors), such as reading Scripture lessons, offering prayer petitions, receiving the candle, or bringing up the gifts of bread and wine. Are you interested in performing any of these? If so, be sure to volunteer early so that everything can be coordinated.

≷ Is there other special work you wish to contribute to this liturgy of baptism, such as playing a musical instrument, making a baptismal scrapbook, or baking bread for communion? Talk with the parents and clergy about your ideas.

≷ Make sure you attend any instructional or rehearsal sessions. Know your role and do your best to understand expectations both during the ceremony and in your new life as godparent. Be willing to practice and ask questions.

〰 The History of Godparents—Part 2: Persecution and New Roles

Jesus described a radical new vision of God's kingdom: a kingdom where servanthood was more important than power, where the lowliest slave girl had the same worth as a mighty ruler, where authentic faith sometimes clashed with the legalistic boundaries of established institutions. As more and more people embraced the teachings of Jesus, the early church grew by leaps and bounds. In biblical times, the decision-maker (usually the husband) could make choices for the entire family, choices that would affect his wife, children, and even his servants. In the sixteenth chapter of Acts, we read about entire families baptized together: Lydia, the seller of purple cloth, was baptized with her entire household; the jailer guarding Paul and Silas brought his whole family to be baptized.

As the early church continued to grow, many leaders from both the religious and political realms vehemently opposed this upside-down vision of a kingdom and sought to retain control by clamping down on anyone who broke the rules. This led to severe persecution of early believers who often lived in dread, meeting in secret places. The constant threat of harassment, imprisonment, or death meant that being baptized was a dangerous declaration of one's beliefs and convictions.

The threat of persecution also meant that new converts introduced an element of risk to the established

Persecution in the Early Church

Stephen is stoned to death	Acts 6:8–8:2
Paul's great conversion	Acts 8:1–4; 9:1–16
Peter's escape from prison	Acts 12:1–18
Paul and Silas in prison	Acts 16:19–40
Nothing can separate us from God	Romans 8:35–39
Put on the "armor of God"	Ephesians 6:10–20
Paul's letter from prison to Corinth	1 Corinthians 4:10–13
Advice to newly baptized being harassed	1 Peter (entire book)
John's visions while imprisoned	Revelation (entire book)

group of believers who were wary that newcomers could betray the community. This gave rise to the official role of baptismal sponsor in the first-century church. Sponsors helped determine the sincerity and trustworthiness of potential candidates. The sponsor had to be willing to stake the life of the entire congregation on the proposition that this candidate was indeed seeking to be a true follower of Christ and not just trying to infiltrate and expose the secret group of Christians. The sponsor acted as surety, guaranteeing the credibility of the new convert, instructing her in this new faith, and welcoming her into the group of believers who would support her new life in Christ.

Adults would study for a year or more, receiving instruction about what it meant to be a follower of Christ and reflecting on the implications of their baptismal commitment. One of the early church fathers wrote, "If any understand the weighty import of baptism, they will fear its reception more than its delay" (Tertullian (193 CE), "On Baptism," ch. 18). The baptismal sponsor helped the newly converted person through this entire process.

⚡ Why Do We Baptize Children?

In today's world, there are many different faith traditions, but one of the things present in all denominations of Christianity is some method of baptism. We may incorporate different details of this sacrament in various ways, but we almost universally agree that baptism is a central symbol of our Christian faith: "One Lord, one faith, one baptism" (Eph 4:5).

Sometimes people from other traditions have a hard time understanding why the Episcopal Church baptizes infants. Many faith groups see baptism as a declaration of *belief*, whereas we see it as a declaration of *belonging*. Infants do not have the intellectual capacity to understand the sacrament, so we acknowledge that they cannot

possibly hold the "right" beliefs, but we baptize them any-
way, because they *belong* here with us. We would never
wait to feed a child until she is able to explain why she
needs food. In the same way children do not have to
understand their need for spiritual sustenance in order to
benefit from the church offering it to them. Furthermore,
when we baptize infants, it is a powerful reminder that
God's grace is freely given to us, it is never earned: An
infant couldn't possibly have performed any good works
to earn God's grace, but nevertheless, grace is generously
lavished upon us. We receive God's grace and we remember once again that God loves us, not for our goodness,
but for our very being.

Baptism initiates and incorporates us into the Body of
Christ, the church. In baptism, we are named and claimed
as a Child of God and made part of God's family. Our
baptism is immediately celebrated by a Christian community who commits to teach us about God and provide
support as we grow into the full stature of Christ. The
community welcomes us by saying, "We receive you into
the household of God. Confess the faith of Christ crucified, proclaim his resurrection, and share with us in his
eternal priesthood" (BCP, 308).

As we grow and learn and are transformed, we
continue to live more fully into our baptismal covenant.
We learn more about the apostles' teaching and the
breaking of bread. We learn that when we fall into sin, we
can repent and return to a God who always stands ready

to forgive and embrace. We learn to proclaim the good news of new and unending life in Christ. We learn to seek and serve Christ in others. We strive for the ideals of justice and peace and try to learn to treat every human being with dignity.

On the Day of Baptism

- ≷ Find a few minutes before you leave for church to say a special prayer of thanksgiving and blessing for your godchild and her parents.
- ≷ Arrive at church early so you can find your seat, get settled, and help the parents with any last-minute details.
- ≷ Read over the church bulletin and pay close attention to any instructions so you will know where to stand and when to speak.
- ≷ Be flexible and gracious about any last-minute changes that might occur.
- ≷ If you bring a camera, be sure to ask about appropriate times for picture taking. Most churches will not want pictures taken during the actual ceremony.
- ≷ When you present your godchild, profess your own beliefs, and make vows on behalf of your godchild, speak loudly and clearly. Make your promises with conviction, before man and God.

We trust that the baptismal vows made on behalf of this child will take root in her heart and encourage her ever-deepening relationship with God. We trust God will continually be revealed in her life and the gathered community will continue to instruct and uphold her new and blossoming faith. We also pray that someday she will reach the place in her journey where she hears her own bell and awakens to a new responsibility, and she chooses to fulfill the vows made by her parents and godparents for her on the day of her baptism.

By welcoming children into our midst from the very beginning of their lives, we are providing a safe space where they can encounter Almighty God and take their rightful place in God's kingdom. Jesus did this same thing in his own ministry:

> People were bringing even infants to him that he might touch them; and when the disciples saw it, they sternly ordered them not to do it. But Jesus called for them and said, "Let the little children come to me, and do not stop them; for it is to such as these that the kingdom of God belongs. Truly I tell you, whoever does not receive the kingdom of God as a little child will never enter it." (Luke 18:15–17)

The people in this story play the same role that parents and godparents play today—they brought the children to Jesus so that he might touch them. Jesus gathered the children to himself, welcoming them into God's kingdom, telling those gathered that the kingdom of God belongs to those who can receive it as a child—with openness, honesty, innocence, and eagerness.

Chapter 2

"I'd Like You to Meet Someone Special"

Getting to Know God

Seeds

"Do you believe in God the Father?
Do you believe in Jesus Christ the Son of God?
Do you believe in God the Holy Spirit?"

One of the great privileges of being a godparent is that you get to plant an important seed: You get to help introduce another human being to God. That seed will grow and blossom into a lifelong relationship with the Creator of the vast universe, who loves each one of us with a particular and infinite love. Love is not just a deep emotional state. It is being committed to someone through thick and thin—through different seasons of life and different emotional states. In the same way, belief in God is not just an intellectual endeavor. It is a commitment to seeking and knowing God—both when there are signs and wonders and when God seems silent. Being in relationship with God is like being in any long-term relationship: It is a conscious act of the will, an act of faith, a commitment to believe.

The commitment to believe in God, to follow Jesus and to accept the Spirit's guidance is a highly personal decision. In baptism, the parents and godparents make a choice to help set a child on a path toward God's kingdom, but at some point, that child will have to decide whether or not he wishes to continue on this path. Each person has the right to make his own choice, but often the preparation that leads up to that choice is best made in partnership with a community. The parents and godparents commit to raise this child in a community of faith that will partner with him and help him learn about God and discover his own faith.

Sharing God's Stories

≋ Read Bible stories together. Talk about their meanings both then and now.

≋ Listen to or sing songs together. Discuss how songs not written specifically about God can still teach us things about God and God's world.

≋ Watch videos about Bible stories. (See www.god parenting.info for recommendations.)

≋ Wonder together about how Jesus looked, what he ate, what he joked about, what he liked to do, etc.

≋ Point out ways the Christian community reflects God's ongoing words and presence.

≋ Talk about things your godchild may hear or memorize from church such as the Lord's Prayer or creeds. Pay attention to words that may seem unclear to a child.

≋ Draw pictures with your godchild or search for symbols that remind you of some aspect of God's nature.

≋ Go to church together and discuss the rituals and symbols we see there. Call ahead of time and see if you can arrange a tour of "behind the scenes."

There are many times when having a partner or companion is really important. Think about how helpful it is to have someone with you when you try something new like visiting an unknown city or when you talk to a doctor about a serious health problem. Think about how much more fun it is to celebrate something joyous like a birthday or an accomplishment with others instead of by yourself. There are also times when safety and common sense tell us we should have another person close by—like a swimming buddy. In the same way, being a Christian is often easier, more fun, and less unsure within a safe community of faith or with a god-partner, which is where godparents come in.

In the baptism ceremony, godparents promise to "be responsible for seeing that the child is brought up in the Christian faith and life" and that by their prayers and witness, they will "help this child to grow into the full stature of Christ" (BCP, 302). You don't ultimately make decisions for your godchild—he will need to do that for himself time and time again as situations arise—but you are there as a partner: helping to plan and guide, ready to celebrate, warning of dangers, and helping him live as a faithful Christian.

Remember you aren't alone in this endeavor. Not only will your godchild have you as a partner to help teach him about God, but God will also be a part of this relationship. God's presence in your life and in the life of your godchild surrounds and intertwines with the fellowship the two of you are building; it is a third distinct dimension to the relationship. God's presence is everywhere, reaching out to us, calling us to God's self at every turn. It is important to remember that while parents and godparents, teachers and mentors all may help nourish this seed of faith, it is God and God alone who is Lord of the Harvest. On days when you feel as if your efforts may not be producing anything, remember that as Christians we are not called to be successful—we are called to be *faithful*. Just keep tending the seed, keep watering and nurturing the tiny sprout that emerges, but trust that God will bring this child to full and complete bloom.

In your enthusiasm to nurture your godchild, don't forget that one of the first obligations of being an effective godparent is to make sure you create space in your own life to recognize God's presence and take time to nurture or renew your own personal relationship with God. After all, you can't introduce your godchild to someone you don't know, right? If you practice having eyes to see God's presence all about you, it will be much easier to point out all those little signs and wonders to your godchild.

Images of God

Abba ("Papa")	Mark 14:36; Romans 8:14–17; Galatians 4:4–7
Advocate/helper	John 14:26; 16:7–15
Breath/Life/Wind	Genesis 1:1–2; John 20:21–22; Acts 2:1–4
Christ	1 John 5:1

Images of God (continued)

Comforter	Psalm 56:8; 86; Matthew 5:4
Creator	Genesis 1:1–2:4a; 2:4b–25
Dove	Matthew 3:16–17
Father	Matthew 6:6–15; 6:25–34; 23:9
Feminine	Genesis 1:27; Deuteronomy 32:18; Isaiah 49:14–15
Fire	Exodus 3:1–6; Acts 2:1–4
Friend	Exodus 33:11; James 2:23; John 15:12–17
Goodness	Psalm 118:1
Guide	John 14:6–14
Healer	Numbers 12:13; Psalm 41; Matthew 14:35–36
Husband/Bridegroom	Isaiah 54:5–8; Hosea 2:14–23; John 3:27–29
Jesus as sibling	Hebrews 2:10–18
Judge	Matthew 25:31–46; Revelation 20:11–15

Images of God (continued)

King	1 Samuel 8:4–9
Lawgiver	Psalm 119
Lord	Deuteronomy 10:17; Isaiah 6:1–5; Romans 10:9
Love	1 John 4:7–8
Messiah	John 1:40–41; Mark 8:27–30
Mother	Isaiah 66:12–13; Matthew 23:37
Partner	John 15:15; Hebrews 3:14
Savior/Redeemer	Luke 1:68–75; 1 Timothy 1:15
Servant	John 13:3–17; Isaiah 52:13–53:12
Shepherd	Psalm 23; Isaiah 40:11
Silence	1 Kings 19:11–13
Spirit	Joel 2:28–29; John 4:23–24; 14:26; Acts 2:1–18
Strength	Jeremiah 1:4–8; Ephesians 6:10–17
Teacher/Rabbi	John 1:35–38; 13:13

⧈ Getting to Know God as Creator and Parent

God as creator wasn't involved just "in the beginning" (Gen 1:1)—God is present in the ongoing, well-ordered complexity of nature. We see creative aspects of God each time we recognize the power of a thunderstorm or the miracle of small flowers that blossom after the rain. We appreciate God's creativity when we gaze at skies painted with the brilliant colors of a sunset or when we notice the uniqueness of each individual snowflake. We honor God's presence in the world by acknowledging that each aspect of nature is good—both in its own right and as it fits with the rest of creation. When we look at the world around us that God has made, we echo the words of Genesis 1:31: ". . . . and indeed, it was very good."

But more than just enjoying God's creation, we are also called to the role of being God's partners in creation. We are an essential part of God's creation and God has given us the special role of cocreator and caregiver. We are to tend creation and take care of it just as wise and kindly rulers would guard their realm (see Gen 1:26–28). Even young godchildren can learn to partner with God as caregivers by recognizing that a flower is pretty, learning to be gentle with pets and helping keep food and water dishes full, assisting in the garden, or being given charge over their own potted plant. Chores are not a burden when we realize that we are part of creation and are doing our part to help God keep it running smoothly. Learning the concept of partnership with God in early childhood sets the stage for a lifetime of interaction with God's creation and can lead to increased awareness and deeper concern about environmental issues as the child matures.

Another reason to help your godchild learn about nature is that it will gently introduce the concept of death as a natural part of the cycle of life. When children plant a seed in bare dirt, we are also teaching them to watch carefully for signs of new life. When the flowers change from the vibrant colors of full bloom to the darker withered colors of death, we have the opportunity to teach children what we believe about the rhythm of the seasons and both how life ends and how life continues. When we see a dead animal by the side of the road, we can share things that make us sad. When we find seashells on the beach, we can talk about how animals left the shell behind and how someday we will leave our bodies behind. Death is a difficult concept for most people to talk about, but part of the role of parents and godparents is to help give children tools of faith to deal with difficult concepts.

In his book *The Road Less Traveled*, M. Scott Peck said, "When we shy away from death, the ever-changing nature of things, we inevitably shy away from life." We don't want our children to shy away from life, we want them to embrace life. If children have observed that both death and birth occur regularly in nature, they have laid some important foundations for when they inevitably have to deal with the death of a relative or friend, or a beloved pet. By seeing the cycles of death and new life in creation, they are also learning about a loving Creator who can be trusted.

One of the easiest ways to begin a conversation with a child about God is to take a walk outside. In the beauty of creation, you'll find plenty of things to inspire spontaneous conversations with your godchild, to plant a seed about the loving God who designed all the marvels of nature. Here are some ideas to get you started:

Finding God Outside

- Plant seeds with your godchild and watch them grow as you both learn to be caretakers.
- Poke toothpicks into sweet potatoes and suspend them over glasses of water so that the ends of the potatoes are submerged. Watch them sprout roots and leaves.
- Take nature walks and look for treasures—keep them in a special box.
- Feed the birds or create a birdfeeder by stringing Cheerios on a piece of yarn.
- Use pictures or photos to make a collage of some miracles you find.

Finding God Outside (continued)

≷ Observe ants or other creatures outside, or purchase an ant farm and continue your observations inside.

≷ Look at intricate patterns in a leaf. Cover the leaf with paper. Gently rub the side of a crayon over the paper to make a leaf impression.

≷ Make a flower wreath or daisy chain, thanking God for flowers as you work.

≷ Set up a recycling station and talk about how we are partners with God and how we can help renew the world.

≷ Getting to Know God as Redeemer and Son

Jesus' life on earth helps us see how involved God can be in our lives. When we remind ourselves that Jesus is fully human *and* fully divine, we realize that God knows what it's like to be human. Jesus was born a human baby with human needs. He was born to humble peasant parents and grew up in a working-class family. Around the age of thirty, he began to share his radical picture of God as a loving parent who longs to be in relationship with us. Jesus proclaimed a message of astonishing, life-changing love and hope and new life, describing a kingdom that didn't look like any kingdom anyone had ever seen before. He lived and worked and walked among the common people, but he did extraordinary things. He healed the sick and loved the unlovable. He shared God with unlikely groups of vagabonds and provoked the religious leaders of his time, challenging them to expand their ideas about God and God's people. His revolutionary words landed him in court, where he was sentenced to death, and still the story continued. He rose from the dead, conquering death for us all, and ascended into heaven, where he is seated at the right hand of the Father. And even after all this time, his message of astonishing, life-changing love and hope and new life lives on. His essence still moves among the people, healing, loving, sharing visions of God and God's kingdom. That's the good news, the gospel— that's what being a Christian is all about.

The Bible tells many stories about Jesus' teaching and miracles but also gives us glimpses into his relationships. Interpersonal encounters are part of what defines our humanity, and you may want to talk with your godchild about the relationships found in Bible stories. Jesus had a family and friends; he attended parties; he prayed intimately both privately and in public; he had interesting discussions with people and wasn't afraid to ask or answer difficult questions. Jesus interacted with both powerful people and the outcasts of society. He valued friendship with women and never underestimated the contribution of children. He enjoyed being with people but also needed time alone. He encountered people who were jealous of him and people who tried to trick him into saying something scandalous. He had associates who didn't understand what he was doing or didn't approve of the way he was doing it. He understood how sometimes friends can share so much and become so close they are like family, and he understood what it feels like to be tragically betrayed by someone you trust.

In all these relationships, Jesus shows us how to turn the other cheek when we are insulted and how to demonstrate compassion to people who scorn and despise us. Time and time again, he offers forgiveness to those who wish to do him harm for speaking the truth. He models for us a life (and a ministry) that was bathed in prayer. By his interactions, Jesus offers a vision of the God who longs to be with us. God came to earth, not as a mighty king, but as a vulnerable baby who had to be held, and cared for, and loved. That baby became an unconventional, energetic boy who grew into a man who talked about the power of Love and created a new awareness of God that turned the world upside down and inside out.

ξ Getting to Know the Preteen Jesus

We only have one story of Jesus in adolescence, so it is important to examine the story of him in the temple:

> Now every year his parents went to Jerusalem for the festival of the Passover. And when he was twelve years old, they

went up as usual for the festival. When the festival was ended and they started to return, the boy Jesus stayed behind in Jerusalem, but his parents did not know it. Assuming that he was in the group of travelers, they went a day's journey. Then they started to look for him among their relatives and friends. When they did not find him, they returned to Jerusalem to search for him. After three days they found him in the temple, sitting among the teachers, listening to them and asking them questions. And all who heard him were amazed at his understanding and his answers. When his parents saw him they were astonished: and his mother said to him, "Child, why have you treated us like this? Look, your father and I have been searching for you in great anxiety." He said to them, "Why were you searching for me? Did you not know that I must be in my Father's house?" But they did not understand what he said to them. Then he went down with them and came to Nazareth, and was obedient to them. His mother treasured all these things in her heart. And Jesus increased in wisdom and in years, and in divine and human favor. (Luke 2:41–52)

Digging into This Story

≳ What do you think Jesus was seeking in the temple?

≳ How would you have felt if you had been Joseph or Mary during those long three days and two nights of looking for Jesus?

Digging into This Story (continued)

≷ What questions do you think Jesus asked the elders?

≷ Have you ever had an adult be "amazed" by you? What did that feel like?

≷ How can other adults see you in ways that perhaps your parents can't?

≷ How can your parents know you in ways that other adults don't?

≷ What do you think Mary cherished about that day?

≷ Getting to Know God as Sustainer and Spirit

The Holy Spirit is the third member of the Trinity, but can sometimes be more difficult to talk about because the Spirit is not a material being, but rather an ever-transforming life force and the very breath of God. We recognize symbols of the Holy Spirit, such as the dove descending during Jesus' baptism or the wind blowing on Pentecost, but a single symbol cannot explain the multifaceted role of the Holy Spirit. The Spirit is sent to sustain us, to be our comforter, our advocate, our counselor. Toward the end of his earthly ministry, Jesus tells his disciples that he will soon have to leave. They are shaken and confused, but Jesus assures them, "I will not leave you comfortless" (John 14:18, KJV) and promises that his Father will send the Holy Spirit.

The Spirit did arrive—and in a most dramatic way. After Jesus ascended into heaven, the disciples were gathered on Pentecost. Suddenly the house was filled with a rushing wind and tongues of fire appeared. The Spirit gave the disciples the ability to speak other languages, making them able to share God's good news with many different people (Acts 2:1–4). Throughout the rest of the New Testament, we read stories of the Spirit moving through groups of new believers, and even today, the Spirit's work continues: comforting, gathering, nurturing, facilitating, creating, supporting, inspiring.

Looking at the tasks and nature of the Holy Spirit, we can see something of the feminine aspects of God's character. In fact, the Hebrew word for "spirit" is *ruach*— a feminine word representing the breath of God. God is neither male nor female, but this does not mean that God is an ambiguous genderless being. Perhaps it is more in keeping with God's nature to imagine God as the embodiment of the very best qualities of both genders. After all, both male and female are reflected in the image of God: "God created humankind in his image, in the image of God he created them; male and female he created them" (Gen 1:27). With this in mind, we can celebrate God as the ultimate depiction of the best masculine traits *and* the best feminine traits.

Writing Your Own Creed

Now that we've looked at the Trinity, it's time to put your faith into your own words. Complete the following phrases to create your own Creed.

I believe in God who

_____

I believe in Jesus who

_____

I believe in the Holy Spirit who

_____

I believe that the church

_____

Now compare your creed to the Apostle's Creed (BCP, 120) and the Nicene Creed (BCP, 358–59). How are they the same? How are they different?

Refer also to the catechism "An Outline of the Faith" (BCP, 845–62) to help understand and explain to your godchild some of the basic beliefs of our church.

Many modern Christians are uneasy talking about the Holy Spirit, afraid that inviting the Spirit in will open the door to unpredictable events or outbursts, but nothing could be further from the truth. God is not a God of confusion (1 Cor 14:33), and when the Spirit is authentically present, there is both order *and* excitement (1 Cor 14:40). We experience God's Spirit in many ways—perhaps you've felt the Holy Spirit when you've been touched by beautiful music, or you've been amazed by how the Scriptures or sermon on a particular day resonate with personal meaning. The Holy Spirit is nothing to be afraid of, so when the Spirit hovers over the waters of baptism, or inspires people to tell the story of Christ in new and imaginative ways, or dances through our worship service or our lives, offering restful words or setting our hearts on fire, we can welcome her without reservation, knowing that the very breath of God is hovering in our midst.

Nancy's Story: Meeting God

I had always wanted to believe in God, to really know God. But the possibility seemed rather remote—something for special people like saints and mystics, not for an ordinary person like me. But I once met a man who showed by his words and actions that he truly believed. It was obvious that he had a relationship with God and it had real impact on how he lived his life. So I asked him if he could introduce me to Jesus. The response I got was actually quite simple:

"My own experience was meeting Jesus in Scripture, in the Holy Land, and in prayer. There I discovered a Jesus who is neither remote nor intimidating. It took me awhile to relax enough in my relationship with him to actually pray without fear. Give it time and keep it up and you may just be surprised." So I took some time to intentionally go "to a deserted place" (Mark 1:35) where I could pray and read Scripture. And God was there, waiting for me.

Although I would often go back to the special place by my mountain, or to a chapel near work, I found myself inviting God to come back with me to my everyday life to help me face whatever challenge had sent me running for help. Eventually I'd also discover God waiting for me around the corner with flowers, or giving me refuge from the world at home. I honestly have not been the same since that first day.

Chapter 3

"What's for Supper?"

Formation, Fellowship, Bread, and Prayers

"Will you continue in the apostles' teaching and fellowship, in the breaking of bread, and in the prayers?"

Have you had a chance to feed your godchild yet? Isn't it a neat experience to hold the bottle and watch how, while the baby is hungry for nourishment, she will reach out and hold your finger? In the early months of life, infants can be fed only milk. It will be awhile before they can chew or digest solid food. In the same way, young children of God will soon become hungry for things beyond the basic human needs of comfort, warmth, and security. How can we feed and form them in ways that help them fully mature?

A child needs many things to grow physically and mentally, and your godchild will also need tools to help her grow spiritually. The apostle Paul wrote to the church in Corinth about being "infants in Christ" and moving from spiritual milk to solid food (1 Cor 3:1–2). You can help your godchild gather some basic building blocks of spiritual development by telling Bible stories and helping her learn the language of our faith. As she matures, you can ask questions to help her delve into the deeper layers of meaning found in our faith stories. By encouraging your godchild to connect her story to the stories of God and God's people, you are helping her stretch her spiritual muscles. By nurturing her spiritual self as well as her physical body, you help her find the balance of Jesus who "grew in wisdom and in years, and in divine and human favor" (Luke 2:52).

Children are learning all the time, soaking up huge amounts of information from the world around them. Children naturally look up to adults and watch us very carefully. What better incentive could there be to put our Christian beliefs into daily practice? Becoming a godparent gives you the chance to refocus some attention on your own spiritual life as you also nurture the spiritual development of your godchild. You may find it helpful to revisit familiar Bible stories or read books on spiritual topics. Consider selecting your own Christian mentor or spiritual director who can guide and support you as you grow into this significant spiritual role in the life of another person.

Assistance can also be found at your local church. Some churches create a "Guild of the Christ Child" to support members by offering baptism instruction, helping parents choose appropriate godparents, providing meals for the family after a child is born, or making banners for the baptism. Some guilds also reach beyond the congregation to help other children in the community. If your local church does not have such a group, you may wish to meet with your clergy or Christian educator to find support, or start a guild yourself.

Part of your responsibility as a godparent is to help your godchild find her place (and voice) in worship. Baptism is the official recognition of a beloved child of God, heir to God's kingdom, and therefore a vital, participating member of your church community. Scripture likens the church to the "Body of Christ," with each member using his or her individual gifts in ways that benefit the entire body (1 Cor 12:12–27). Using the metaphor of a body is a great way to talk with children about different roles. It can help children recognize the gifts God has given them and discern how their gifts might be of service in God's family.

One gift you as a godparent can share with your godchild is to help her understand how she can "continue in the apostles' teaching and fellowship, in the breaking of bread, and in the prayers" (BCP, 304). As you model for her this covenantal promise, you continue your own spiritual growth. The journey you embark on with your godchild is *your* journey too. It's never too late to begin (or begin again). You just might be amazed by how much you learn about your own faith along the way. (For more in-depth study on the "covenant of baptism," see Nancy's book *Do You Believe? Living the Baptismal Covenant*, Morehouse Publishing, 2006.)

⚡ The Apostles' Teaching

We are formed by many things: the influence of our parents, the environment in which we live, the interests and skills we develop, the choices we make, and the list goes on. Likewise, our spiritual selves are formed from a complex web of ideas, emotions, and experiences. We are also formed by elements of the apostles' teaching and our denominational traditions, such as music, worship, prayers, Scripture, and creeds.

Over the last few years there has been much discussion in religious education circles about formation vs. education. To offer a quick definition: Education is "book stuff"; formation is everything else. Episcopalians are sometimes called "people of the book" because of our close ties with the Book of Common Prayer—we are educated by its liturgies and prayers. We also learn from stories and principles in the Bible and even from our hymns. Education is probably what you think of in a traditional Sunday school program for children, but formation is something very different.

If education represents "book stuff," then formation is everything else—or perhaps more precisely it's how you allow the book stuff and everything else to shape and transform you. Formation happens through relationships we build, people we observe, colors and symbols we see in church, emotions that arise from music, or prayers we learn. Formation happens in hundreds of ways. Education is *one* way in which formation happens, but it is not the *only* way. In truth, it is probably not even the primary way. The good news is we don't have to choose between education and formation. In true Anglican fashion, we don't have to choose "either/or"—we can celebrate "both/and." We need book knowledge—concrete facts, chronicled history of how we got here, stories of our faith, ancient prayers, and the creeds, but we also need to soar beyond

Learning through Sacred Play

≋ Talk with your godchild about what she sees, hears, tastes, touches, and feels in church.

≋ Spend time "playing church" with your godchild. (Dolls and well-behaved teddy bears are welcome too.) Sing songs, encourage her to read or tell Bible stories, talk about what happens in church.

≋ For a special gift, consider investing in some play materials for your godchild that will help her think about church and God while at home. (For specific recommendations visit www.godparenting.info.)

≋ If you are living in the same city as your godchild, you may wish to sign up to help in her Sunday school class. You can also make short-term commitments like helping with Vacation Bible School or being a guest speaker.

≋ Help your godchild understand and memorize the words of the Nicene Creed. This ancient creed is the basic statement of belief, but as one Episcopal bishop put it, it is also "a syllabus of the topics with which faithful people wrestle." (Tracey says: Thanks to The Rt. Rev. J. Neil Alexander, Bishop of the Episcopal Diocese of Atlanta, who offered these life-changing words of wisdom to me. His approach invited me into deeper conversation with, and understanding of, the ancient creeds and made it safe to ask my questions. I hope you will find the same.)

Learning through Sacred Play (continued)

- Talk with your godchild about God's kingdom and the principles of love, justice, forgiveness, peace, and acceptance. Play "kingdom" games with your godchild. Castles and horses are okay, but also incorporate God as loving king and mystical spiritual guide, Christians as fellow citizens, and Jesus as beloved son and rescuing savior.

the printed page. We need to let those words actually catch fire in our souls and change our world from the inside out.

Many new godparents worry they don't have enough Bible knowledge or religious experience to truly educate their godchild, but that's okay, your local parish can help with education. Often a godparent's most significant contribution is helping with formation—as you ask or listen to questions, or talk about your own faith, you are nurturing the relationship with your godchild and helping form her as a Christian.

Fellowship

Fellowship, as defined by the American Heritage Dictionary, is "the close association of individuals sharing similar interests, ideals, or experiences in a congenial atmosphere and on equal terms." In the church, "on equal terms" means we need to include children in authentic fellowship. Relationships are always two-way streets, and children have their own contributions to make.

Children have a unique relationship with God, and they need adults to listen, value, and affirm that. Help your godchild find her individual place in the fellowship of believers. Remind her (and others) that when we break bread—either in sharing a meal or around the communion table—children are an essential part of our community. Without children, our circle is incomplete.

As a godparent, you share fellowship not just with your faith community, but also with your godchild's family. Perhaps you helped prepare for your godchild's birth, but now you add a new dimension as you build a personal fellowship with this child by spending time together forming and nurturing your relationship. As a spiritual role model, you can talk about God, faith, church, or whatever your godchild needs to discuss.

Some visits with your godchild will be just for fun— a walk, a trip to the zoo, or a picnic enjoying God's creation. But as your godchild grows, the relationship is growing too, and that fun foundation can provide safe space for her to wrestle with questions, giving voice to doubts or fears as they arise, and sharing insights as they are discovered. She may confide in you or ask for your advice. In those moments, take a deep breath, pray for guidance, and offer caring responses. Ask yourself, "What would God, loving and merciful, say to this child?"

Enjoying Fellowship with Your Godchild

≳ Spend time together. If you don't live close by, make "phone dates" or write regular emails or letters. Make sure your godchild knows how to get in touch with you if she needs you.

≳ Ask questions that leave open space for your godchild to offer her own contributions: "What do you think about . . ." or "I've always wondered about . . ."

≳ If possible, attend some church functions with your godchild. Choose a special service like the Easter Vigil and make it an annual event.

≳ Receive communion with your godchild, sharing in the Eucharistic feast, and celebrating new life in Christ.

≳ Become an advocate for child-friendly worship and fellowship that meets the needs of many ages "on equal terms."

≳ Drive or walk with your godchild to church, using the quiet one-on-one time as an opportunity to catch up, listen to questions, or just talk about what's happening in her life.

≳ Talk to your godchild. Ask questions and listen to the answers. Encourage her to ask her own questions. As she gets older, share some of your own ideas and beliefs, as well as those things you question and wonder about.

Destiny's Story: Finding Fellowship

Several years ago my grade-school-age son, Jason, and I joined the Episcopal Church. We attended for several months and then I was officially "received." This was the Christian community experience I had been looking for. Shortly after that my son asked if he could be baptized.

The godparents we chose for him were people in our new congregation who had already begun to embrace and sponsor him. Two were Sunday school teachers who often volunteered to take him to church activities when I, as a single mom, could not. Another was an active church member who always found something for Jason to do when he wanted to volunteer at church and never once said, "You're too young."

Jason was truly adopted by these people and their extended families. He went on overnight church camp retreats with one family and was referred to as a "godbrother" by the children of one of his godparents.

Although Jason is an adult now and living in another state, these people are still important to him. They were the Christians who were there to nourish him when he needed them most.

The Breaking of Bread

When Episcopalians talk about communion, we often use the word "Eucharist," which comes from the Greek word "*eucharistia*," meaning "thanksgiving." Baptism is the formal welcome into God's family, but the Eucharist is the ongoing thanksgiving for, and renewal of, that relationship. When the community of faith gathers to share Eucharist, we experience communion—in every sense of the word. The Eucharistic feast is highly symbolic, but the two primary symbols are bread and wine.

Bread is a basic unifier across families and cultures. It is a universal symbol of hearth and home, of nourishment and care. When we share bread, we share life, making this an appropriate metaphor for Christ's body, the church. Baking bread is like building community. There's nothing artificial in homemade bread—it's all very organic. It's a tactile, hands-on activity—you can't be uninvolved; you have to get your hands in it, monitor each step, and possibly adjust your plan as you go. You combine ingredients and knead the dough over and over again, working at blending various ingredients into one seamless whole. It's not a process where you control every aspect: After you've kneaded the dough and done your part, you have to wait and give the yeast time to do its work. You can't hurry—it takes whatever time it takes; if you rush the process, the end result may suffer. After the dough rises, the bread bakes and fills your home with a warm, inviting smell that draws people in. When we enjoy this food we helped create, we are thankful it can provide temporary physical sustenance, but we also remind ourselves that the Bread of Life is the only true source of eternal life. We remember we cannot live without ongoing nourishment, and we offer thanks to Jesus the Bread of Life: "You are the source of Life. Without you, I could not survive." (See John 6:32–40.)

Wine represents the cup of the new covenant (1 Cor 11:25) and is the symbol of Christ's blood and sacrifice. Some churches use grape juice in communion, but the Episcopal Church chooses to use wine. The wonder of wine happens when grapes are grown, harvested, crushed, and fermented. Both grape juice and wine can be a deep red-purple color that reminds us of the vital sacrifice made for us, but we believe there is something truly essential and life-giving about using *wine* as our symbol. In Scripture, we read about wine in stories of feasting and celebration, a symbol of God's blessing and prosperity. There are numerous Scripture passages about wine—as a blessing (Isa 65:8), as an offering (Exod 29:40–41), and even as a sign of gladness (Ps 104:14–15). The Eucharist is a mysterious, even risky, drama of change and celebration, and somehow grape juice just doesn't carry that same weight. In his book *Wishful Thinking: A Seeker's ABC*, Frederick Buechner says: "Wine is booze, which means it is dangerous and drunk-making. It makes the timid brave and the reserved amorous. It loosens the tongue and breaks the ice especially when served in a loving cup. It kills germs. As symbols go, [wine] is a rather splendid one. . . . There's nothing dangerous or intoxicating or complex about grape juice."

Finding God in Bread

≈ Bake bread with your godchild and talk about the significance of communion bread, as well as bread used in other Bible stories. Eat the bread at a shared meal.

≈ Give thanks to God for your godchild as you watch her eating and growing. Be sure to supply meals that nourish both body and soul.

≈ If someone in your godchild's family is sick, you may want to bring the family a meal. Depending on the traditions of your church, you may also wish to talk with the clergy about bringing communion.

≈ Have a tea party or picnic with your godchild. Remember, you can invite God and the angels to all your meals.

≈ Show your godchild how we care for others. Collect and deliver food to people in need. Give food certificates or warm socks to homeless people.

≈ Read the book of Ruth together, noticing the importance of grain. Look for a local gleaning group— groups who gather and contribute to food banks whatever is left in the fields after the farmers have harvested their crops.

≈ As your godchild gets older, discuss the gift of wine, its symbolism, and the importance of enjoying it responsibly.

Finding God in Bread (continued)

≋ During an extended visit with your godchild, you may want to talk about and practice the spiritual discipline of fasting. Explain how people use this discipline to enhance their prayer life or prepare for something important.

≋ Attend a Seder/Passover meal together. Discuss how Jesus celebrated this ancient Jewish ritual, and how it is a part of our heritage as well.

As we honor the symbols of communion, we teach our children to be thankful to God, much the same way we offer thanks before meals. During the Eucharist, we are invited to God's table to remember the sacrifices made for us. We remind ourselves that all good things—bread and wafers, wine and grape juice, and each other—come from God and are to be shared in community, and we recognize that we all have important roles in God's family—even the youngest members.

≋ Why We Allow Children to Take Communion

When we baptize children, we welcome them into God's family, just as they have been welcomed into our individual families. It may be years before children understand the history or values of their human family, but they are nonetheless significant members of that family. Likewise, in church children may not understand all the mysteries of communion (who does?), but they are learning how the Family of God breaks bread together and receives strength for the journey.

Because the Episcopal Church believes Baptism is a full initiation into the church (BCP, 298), we welcome children of all ages to join as full participants in the Eucharistic feast. In fact, sometimes newly baptized babies are given a tiny drop of consecrated wine, from the tip of the priest's finger, in celebration of their new status as members of the church. Even before infants can chew solid food, they are brought forward to share our communion with Christ and given a special blessing. As they watch, they learn something very special is happening that others seem to think is important, and they want to be included. When the child, however young, reaches out for the bread, she is responding to God's invitation. God's invitation extends to all of us, and so the Episcopal Church practices open communion, which means that whatever Christian tradition the godparents (and other guests) come from, they are welcome to receive communion. Sharing communion is one more way to deepen the relationship of godparent and godchild.

You can help your godchild prepare for communion by discussing it first. Explain what the Eucharist means to you. You might use the idea that while food gives nourishment to our bodies, the Eucharist gives nourishment to our whole selves. Explain how we remember Christ's life and how we believe Christ is truly present when we "do this in remembrance of him." Show your godchild how to hold out her hands to receive bread. Teach her about taking a sip of wine or dipping the bread into the cup. Encourage her to say "Amen" (meaning "so be it") after she receives, or how to cross her arms over her chest to signify she is not receiving but would like a blessing. If you need help, talk to parents, clergy, or a local Christian educator.

Debra's Story: Recognizing Jesus in the Breaking of the Bread

When I was the vicar of a small church in Connecticut, there was a three-year-old boy, Jeffrey, who came to the altar rail week after week with his mother. Even after many conversations about why children are included in Eucharist, Jeffrey's mother was reluctant to allow him to receive the sacrament "until he was old enough to understand." Week after week, the little boy would extend his hands to receive, and week after week the mother would pull his hands back to his chest with a thump. But one Sunday, Jeffrey was not to be denied. He extended his hands. His mother pulled them back. Not once but three times— thump, thump, thump.

And then it happened: Jeffrey yelled at the top of his lungs, "Jesus, Jesus! I want Jesus too! Give me Jesus!" and thrust his hands forward again to receive the host.

You could have heard a pin drop. The Spirit silently danced throughout the church. I looked at Jeffrey's mom, both our eyes brimming with tears. She nodded her consent. I barely choked out the words "The Body of Christ" as Jeffrey took Jesus into his hands and pronounced a loud "Amen!" for all to hear. All around the church people were smiling and dabbing their eyes. Jeffrey knelt in awe before Jesus that day, and we were each filled with awe as we searched our own hearts and shared his experience.

(Thanks to The Rev. Debra J. Kissinger who provided this story. She is a missioner to children and child advocate in the Diocese of Bethlehem. A version of this story also appeared in Episcopal Life.)

God's Words about Bread in Scripture

Manna and water in the desert	Exodus 16
Eating in God's presence	Deuteronomy 14:22–29
Generosity is rewarded	1 Kings 17:8–16
Angel brings Elijah bread	1 Kings 19:1–8
Good gifts from God	Matthew 7:7–11
Jesus' last supper	Matthew 26:26–27
Young girl healed and fed	Mark 5:22–24, 35–43
Disciples eating grain on Sabbath	Luke 6:1–5

God's Words about Bread in Scripture (continued)	
Parable of the great banquet	Luke 14:15–24
Risen Jesus eats with disciples	Luke 24:13–35
Jesus' first miracle is at a wedding party	John 2:1–12
Boy helps feed five thousand	John 6:1–15
Jesus as Bread of Life	John 6:32–59
Milk and solid food for believers	1 Corinthians 3:1–4

⌇ The Prayers

For many people, learning to pray is very difficult. It can be especially daunting for those in liturgical traditions who are used to reading beautiful prayers out of prayer books. When we explore the Book of Common Prayer, we find prayers that were lovingly crafted by poets and theologians, and have been around for thousands of years. These are prayers that have been checked for spelling and grammatical errors, and they don't include "um," or "I don't know what to say," or "I have no idea what I'm doing."

Learning to pray is not always easy, but it is important, and here is where you may be able to learn *from* your godchild. Children instinctively understand talking to God. Whereas adults may feel self-conscious or unsure, children are confident and funny and free. They talk to God as they might naturally talk to a friend. Talk with your godchild about prayer and practice some short prayers together.

You may also want to help your godchild memorize the Lord's Prayer so she can better participate in "corporate worship," worship we do with other people. Read each line of the prayer together, focusing on God as heavenly Father, realizing that God's kingdom exists wherever God's will is done, knowing God will give what is needed, recognizing our faults and being forgiving to others, asking for protection, and recognizing God as the ultimate power. Give examples from daily life to help your godchild identify with unfamiliar words. When your godchild understands the full meaning of our repeated prayers, it helps give voice to distinctive prayers of her own as well.

Finding God in Prayer

- ≋ Pray with, for, and about your godchild.
- ≋ Teach your godchild blessings or prayers for mealtime and bedtime.
- ≋ Help older godchildren understand and memorize the Lord's Prayer.

Finding God in Prayer (continued)

≷ Introduce your godchild to different forms of prayer—quiet meditation, dance, songs or chants, reading from books, spontaneous conversation, walking a labyrinth, using prayer beads or prayer flags, or knitting a prayer shawl.

≷ Light candles with your godchild to remind you of God's concern for special intentions.

≷ Give gifts that encourage prayer like a special prayer bell or prayer flags, or children's books about prayer, such as Anytime Prayers by Madeleine L'Engle or The Lord's Prayer illustrated by Tim Ladwig. (See www.godparenting.info for more suggestions.)

≷ For older godchildren, give a special blank journal that can be used to record thoughts, dreams, prayers, questions, and special Scriptures.

≷ Create special prayer rituals, such as quick "Arrow Prayers" (see Channing's Story) that you can send flying when you hear a siren or see a homeless person, such as "God, be with those who need you."

Channing's Story: Arrow Prayers

When I went to boarding school as a child, I learned about "arrow prayers." The point of an arrow prayer is that you don't have to be in a formal setting to pray nor do you need to be elaborate to get God's attention, nor do you need to resort to the Book of Common Prayer. Simply loose the prayer like an arrow.

We were taught a little trinity of arrow prayers for first thing in the morning: "I praise my God this day. I give myself to God this day. I ask my God to help me this day." I find arrow prayers particularly helpful as an alternative to cursing a driver that just cut me off in traffic. It may range from "God, restore my quiet" to "God, help him to get home safely." Once you learn this prayer method, you may be surprised by how often you can use it.

(Thanks to The Rev. R. Channing Johnson who provided this story. He attended the Kent School in Connecticut from 1941–1946. The school was founded by Father Sill of the Order of the Holy Cross, an Episcopal Benedictine Order.)

There are many ways to help your godchild experience formation, fellowship, bread, and prayers. As your relationships with both God and your godchild develop, you will find numerous opportunities to make connections between the activities of your daily life and these foundational concepts of God's kingdom.

Chapter 4

"Gotta Get Washed Up"

Whenever You Fall . . .

"Will you persevere in resisting evil, and, whenever you fall into sin, repent and return to the Lord?"

When children are baptized, they are welcomed as full members in the family of God. We make the sign of the cross on their foreheads and assure them, "You are sealed by the Holy Spirit in Baptism and marked as Christ's own for ever" (BCP, 308). What an amazing gift to offer our children. This powerful symbol assures us that no matter how far we wander, we have been "marked as Christ's own forever," and there is no path we can ever find ourselves on that could take us outside the realm of God's attention and concern.

As our children grow and learn, they will become independent. They will wander. They will learn to make choices and they will sometimes make wrong choices. They will, willingly and unwillingly, hurt other people. They will be hurt—by other people and sometimes just by the circumstances of life. They will be exposed to things we wish they would never see. In short, they will experience the brokenness of living in a world where sin exists.

One of the harder aspects of being a godparent is that we sometimes get asked difficult questions and so we may have to explain the concepts of sin and evil. It is tempting to present your godchild with a simplistic version of the Christian faith where things are black and white: Everyone is good or bad; the good guys always win and the bad guys are always caught, repentant and reformed. But when we teach (even by implication) that the Christian life mostly works out the way we planned it—

that "God's in his heaven, all's right with the world"—
we offer our children only a sugar-coated shell of the
life-changing faith that people have died for. While this
sugar-coated shell may be pretty and very convenient, it
is brittle and weak and utterly unreliable. The reality is
that someday something difficult and terrible and hard is
going to happen in the life of this child you love so much.
When that day comes, he will need something solid to
lean on. If all he has been given is a sugar-coated shell, it
will shatter into pieces at the first sign of real suffering,
leaving him sitting among the shards of an irretrievably
broken mirage with nothing substantial to hold on to.

A better alternative is to help children build a strong,
authentic faith that can stand the test of time. Invariably,
this is a slower and more complicated process than giving
quick, simple solutions. It means carefully considering
difficult questions and admitting that some things are
unknowable. Telling your godchild, "I don't understand it
either" gives you both an opportunity to do some research
or at least have further discussions about complex issues.
Building an authentic faith happens step-by-step, in
fits and starts, but over time you lay a solid foundation.
Perhaps it begins with just a simple assertion such as "God
is good," or "I know that God loves us," or "I believe God
is here." When something terrible happens, you still won't
have a fully satisfying explanation, but you will have given
your godchild (and yourself) a piece of solid ground upon
which to build.

Intentionally thinking about what you believe, and why, can be difficult work. Inevitably, we run into something that makes us think, "I'm just not sure I believe that," and that's okay. It's one of the gifts of being part of a church that practices corporate worship. If you find yourself stumbling over words in creeds or prayers that have always been familiar and comfortable, but suddenly seem prickly or mysterious, being part of corporate worship gives you time to wrestle with it, while other people around you carry the weight of it for a while. Our worship is not dependent on one person's emotional response; worship goes on, even while you struggle. Whatever questions you ask, whatever conclusions you come to, the ongoing worship of the church will be right here waiting for you. If you find yourself in a barren place among the crumbled foundations of everything you ever believed, look a little harder and you can also find the miraculous gift of other believers willing to stand in the gap for you until you get it sorted out with God's help.

Sherry's Story: Standing in the Gap

It was the custom of our church to visit the homes of families planning to have a child baptized. One visit I hold particularly dear was to a young couple who had just had their first child. Over coffee, we talked with the parents and godparents. We reviewed the service, explained where everyone was to stand, what questions would be asked, and what the responses signified. Everyone listened attentively and then the mother asked: "What is our part after the actual baptism? What are we supposed to do for our son until he is old enough to understand these concepts? We have chosen godparents who are ready to help, but none of us really know what to do."

No one said anything for a moment or two. Then I recalled having similar thoughts when my own children were born, and I began to share what God has taught me about the spiritual responsibilities in parenting: "Our job as parents is to share our faith with our children. However, we have to remember that children will be watching and absorbing things from us long before we get to explain what we believe and why, so we do our best to offer a good example of Christianity in action.

"Right now, you have this tiny baby who can't articulate even a basic understanding of who God is or what faith is about, but someday he will. For right now, your job is to 'stand in the gap.' You are the bridge through whom your children will experience God. Part of being a parent or godparent is learning how to quietly stand in the gap, trusting God, because these gaps of time are not only going to happen in the early years of life. In fact, there will be gaps all along the way, including the teenage years and beyond."

When there is a gap in the understanding of a child, he needs people willing to stand in that gap, people who become a bridge—giving him support as he moves from a lack of understanding to the first initial steps of new growth. Your godchild needs something solid on which to stand, someone to stand in the gap, until he can find his own way to a place of firmer understanding. One of the mysteries of parenting is our responsibility to remain in the gap for as long as is needed, graciously moving aside when the child makes his way to where you are; celebrating his growth and progress, but always being ready to stand in the next gap, if or when the need arises.

This idea of standing in the gap has given me great comfort over the years and I believe it is one of the greatest privileges ever given to me as a parent. In my mind I have been given a crystal clear picture that I treasure beyond words: It is the picture of me holding tightly onto God with one hand and holding tightly the hand of my child in the other.

⅀ Resisting Evil

In the baptismal covenant, after we affirm our beliefs about God and vow to continue our formation, we are asked a difficult question, "Will you persevere in resisting evil, and, whenever you fall into sin, repent and return to the Lord?" and without more than a couple microseconds of time to consider, we cheerfully reply: "I will, with God's help."

Have you ever been startled by the starkness of this question? Have you given serious consideration to how difficult it is to live this promise in your daily life? Questions about evil and sin are at the heart of the Christian faith and have been argued by theologians since the beginning of time. And now we ask the parents and godparents to enter into these murky waters to have this conversation with their children.

Forming a personal theology, a structure of understandings about God, is a complex task. We take what we read in Scriptures, hear from tradition, and experience in our own lives, and we try to weave together strands of belief that we can really stake our lives on. This is personal theology at its most real: Defining tenets of faith we believe, not just because we heard it from a pulpit or read it in a book, but something we believe with every fiber of our being because the absolute *Truth* of it resonates in our very bones. If we recognize that forming these kinds of absolute beliefs is a challenging task for even the most mature and well-versed Christian, then we also face the fact that helping our godchildren wrestle with serious theological topics in age-appropriate ways feels almost impossible. No wonder so many adults are tempted to resort to simplistic clichés.

Talking about evil is important, and giving your godchild tools for facing and rejecting evil is a smart and responsible thing to do. But *how do* we talk to children about evil and how to resist it?

Years ago the word "evil" was commonly used to describe both familiar vices like "the evils of alcohol" and behaviors seen as morally wrong or offensive. Even in modern vocabulary, the Merriam-Webster dictionary lists among its definitions for evil: "inferior, disagreeable, causing discomfort or marked by misfortune." Look at our daily news and you may even hear the word "evil" used in conjunction with some current world tensions.

Is this really a definition of evil we are willing to accept? We need to be more careful with our words. True evil isn't represented by things that cause us discomfort or things we find disagreeable. Evil isn't easily described or defined. It isn't a caricature of a man in a red suit with horns and a pitchfork. Evil is a breathtakingly powerful force, bigger than any one person. True evil is something so incomprehensible, so horrible that it actually acts like a vacuum: It is the complete antithesis, or absolute absence, of good.

Talking about evil is messy, disturbing work, but it is important to talk with children about evil when the question comes up. However, we can't end the discussion with evil and just leave it there, because God didn't leave it there. It's easy to get stuck here, however, because, in some ways, we are still living in a Good Friday world—we still live with evil; we still experience pain, brokenness, and death in our world. But—here's where the story gets life-changingly exciting—we are an Easter people! Evil and death may have their day but know what happens on Sunday: Easter is coming! Don't give up hope, never give up hope. God is with us, and this story isn't over.

≷ Ceremony for Rejecting Evil

During the Episcopal baptismal ceremony, candidates are asked, "Do you renounce Satan and all the spiritual forces of wickedness that rebel against God? Do you renounce the evil powers of this world. . . .?" (BCP, 302). These words may sound strange to our ears today, but this part of the baptismal ritual was shaped and established when the newly forming church lived with persecution and the presence of evil shadowed many aspects of daily life. In the early rite new members were told to face west, the direction of darkness, stretch out their hands, to symbolize "Stop!" physically rejecting evil's power and influence. Here are some suggestions to help you recreate this powerful ritual with your godchild.

- ≷ Talk with your godchild about God's goodness and love. Explain that evil is that which draws us away from God or prevents us from being truly loving.

- ≷ Decide on a symbol for God—perhaps a candle, Bible, or a picture of Jesus, and place it toward the east.

- ≷ Next carefully talk about symbols that might represent the evils, sins, or fears you both are currently facing. Perhaps a rock can symbolize a jealous or angry heart, or a dark cloth could represent fear, or you might draw pictures to illustrate negative situations. The symbol(s) chosen for evil are then placed toward the west. (Be careful in this step, as we don't want to reject snakes or big sisters when the real problems may actually be lack of health or absence of harmony.)

≋ Ask your godchild to stand first facing the negative symbol you have chosen, with hands upraised like "Stop!" in rejection. The symbol for God is at his back. Remind your godchild that God is always there "to back him up."

≋ Use the Book of Common Prayer (pp. 302–3) and ask the following questions. (You may want to review together the entire ceremony informally beforehand. You could change some unclear wording, but even young children will enjoy using the actual words from the official book that was used during their own baptism ceremony.)

> *Question* Do you renounce Satan and all the spiritual forces of wickedness that rebel against God?
>
> *Answer* I renounce them.
>
> *Question* Do you renounce the evil powers of this world which corrupt and destroy the creatures of God?
>
> *Answer* I renounce them.
>
> *Question* Do you renounce all sinful desires that draw you from the love of God?
>
> *Answer* I renounce them. (BCP, 302)

≋ Now ask your godchild to turn his back on "evil" and turn toward the east, the direction of the rising sun, and his symbol for God in order to pledge himself personally to Christ.

≋ As your godchild turns toward God's symbol, have him stand tall and proud as you continue:

> *Question* Do you turn to Jesus Christ and accept him as your Savior?
>
> *Answer* I do.
>
> *Question* Do you put your whole trust in his grace and love?
>
> *Answer* I do.
>
> *Question* Do you promise to follow and obey him as your Lord?
>
> *Answer* I do. (BCP, 302–3)

≋ If possible follow up this ritual immediately with some concrete expression of reconciliation or loving action for the sake of God's kingdom, to show that Christianity is not just words, but involves commitment and action as well.

≋ This ritual is especially appropriate if your godchild wants or needs to make amends. You can explain how we recommit ourselves over and over again to follow Christ and the Christian ideals.

≋ God Allows U-Turns

The Book of Common Prayer defines sin as "the seeking of our own will instead of the will of God, thus distorting our relationship with God, with other people, and with all creation" (BCP, 848). Sin is about broken relationships, about that which separates us from God. When we allow sinfulness or brokenness to keep us from fully connecting with God or other people, we leave room for more subtle evils to worm their way into our everyday lives. We might let ourselves be disagreeable or unkind to someone. We might say something hurtful to someone else. We might deliberately close our eyes to an opportunity where we could help. Evil may be a force of darkness outside ourselves, but if we aren't careful—if we don't resist it—it can creep into our life when we are too tired, too overwhelmed, or just too lazy to fight it off.

Repenting of sin is more than just saying, "I'm sorry." It is an ongoing process of connecting and reconnecting. If sin is about shutting ourselves away from God, then repentance is about deliberately changing direction. Repentance is a U-turn, much like the ceremony described above; we choose to turn from focusing on evil to focusing on God. We make a renewed commitment to stay in relationship with the God who loves us and is willing to forgive us, set our sin aside and rebuild the relationship.

Children are often more skilled in forgiveness and reconnection than adults. Have you ever watched children play? Feelings get hurt and tears are shed. Sometimes arguments erupt and games are stopped. But many times, if left alone, children will work it out. Even if someone storms off, or angry words are exchanged, it doesn't take long before everyone is laughing again. We need to learn children's ways of forgiving and be willing to move on, go back, or start over. Think how different our relationships, our churches, and our world would be if adults could learn to reconnect as easily as children do. When we choose to remain apart and hold a grudge, or insist that we are completely right and someone else is completely wrong, we hold ourselves back from sharing who we are, and our relationships are further ripped apart, our communion is disrupted, and we keep ourselves from getting back in the game and getting on with the work God has given *all* of us to do.

A Conversation of Love

The "love chapter" from the book of First Corinthians is one of the best-known passages in Scripture. It is often read at weddings and quoted in sermons, because it is a celebration of authentic relationships. We offer this two-voice setting of the passage as a way for you to read the familiar passage with your godchild. We suggest you read it through twice, so that both people can experience each voice.

If I speak in the tongues of mortals and of angels,
> *but do not have love,*
I am a noisy gong or a clanging cymbal.

And if I have prophetic powers,
and understand all mysteries and all knowledge,
and if I have all faith, so as to remove mountains,
> but do not have love,
> *I am nothing.*

If I give away all my possessions,
and if I hand over my body so that I may boast,
 but do not have love,
I gain nothing.

Love is patient	Love is kind
Love is not envious	or boastful
or arrogant	or rude.

It does not insist on its own way.

It is not irritable   *or resentful*

It does not rejoice in wrongdoing,
 but rejoices in the truth.

It bears all things	*believes all things*
Hopes all things	*endures all things.*

Love never ends.

But as for prophecies	they will come to an end
As for tongues	they will cease
As for knowledge	it will come to an end.

When I was a child	I spoke like a child
I thought like a child	I reasoned like a child
When I became an adult	I put an end to childish ways.

For now we see in a mirror, dimly,
But then we will see face to face.
Now I know only in part   then I will know fully
Even as I have been fully known.

And now faith, hope, and love abide,   *these three*
and the greatest of these is love.

(1 Corinthians 13:1–8, 11–13)

⚡ The Water of Baptism

Water is an amazing gift of life and a wonderful symbol for repenting and returning. Water touches almost every area of our lives. It is used to quench thirst, irrigate crops, heat our homes, cook our food, and clean all kinds of things. Water is also our primary symbol of baptism and therefore a powerful symbol of repentance and renewal. The apostle Peter addressed the crowd: "Repent, and be baptized, every one of you in the name of Jesus Christ so that your sins may be forgiven; and you will receive the gift of the Holy Spirit" (Acts 2:38).

Think about how water affects so many things. It can be energizing to jump into a nice hot shower after a long day—the water washes off the grime and muck of just being in the world, and helps you feel awake and alive. Soaking in a steaming bath soothes aching muscles and relieves stress. On a hot summer day, nothing feels as good as drinking a cold cup of water, unless perhaps it is diving into a cool clear pool that shocks you into new awareness and moves you into a new world. The waters of baptism do all these things too. Baptism ceremonially removes the grime of the world and gives you a sense of new life. It diminishes our pain and brokenness. It revives and refreshes and moves us into a new kind of world.

God's Words about Water

Waters of creation	Genesis 1:1–8
Noah's ark and the great flood	Genesis 6:8–9:17
A well in the desert	Genesis 21:14–21
Rebekah chosen because she offers water	Genesis 24:12–27
Parting of the Red Sea	Exodus 14:1–31
Moses strikes rock for water	Exodus 17:1–7
Soldiers chosen by how they drink water	Judges 7:2–8
Water does not stop Elijah's offering	1 Kings 18:21–40
Jonah and the great fish	Jonah 1:1–2:10
Jesus baptized by John in the river	Mark 1:1–11
Jesus calls disciples by the sea	Mark 1:16–19
Jesus turns water into wine	John 2:1–11
Jesus walks on water, Peter also tries	Matthew 14:22–33
Jesus calms the sea	Luke 8:22–25
Jesus talks to woman about living water	John 4:5–15
Jesus heals near pool	John 5:1–9

God's Words about Water (continued)

Woman washes Jesus' feet with tears	Luke 7:36–50
Jesus washes disciples' feet	John 13:3–7
Pilate washes his hands of Jesus' fate	Matthew 27:24
Blood and water flow from Jesus' side	John 19:34
Disciples recognize risen Lord while fishing	John 21:1–14

Finding God in Water

Children love to play with water and you can use any number of different water games or activities to help your godchild understand the significance of baptism.

- ≷ Create blessing prayers for water as it is used every day—bath time, washing dishes, cleaning scraped knees, drinking, swimming, watering the garden, or prayers for rain.

- ≷ When possible, stand with your godchild at the baptismal font and offer a quick prayer, such as "Thank you, God, for my godson, Tyler." Dip your fingers in the water and make the sign of the cross, remembering the baptism.

≋ Decorate small watering cans with baptismal symbols to remind us how the waters of baptism can nourish new growth.

≋ Visit the ocean or other bodies of water and thank God for all the ways that water sustains life. Give your godchild a shell as a reminder of his baptism.

≋ Mix up a quick bubble solution (1 cup of water, 2 tablespoons glycerin or light Karo syrup, 4 tablespoons dishwashing liquid) and as you blow bubbles with your godchild, talk about how Christians who have the waters of baptism and the breath of the Holy Spirit can soar to unimaginable places.

≋ Use other water activities such as swimming or visiting an aquarium as an occasion to mark the baptism anniversary of your godchild.

≋ Act out a baptism with your godchild using a doll. Have your godchild choose a name for the baby and use a shell or small cup to pour water over the doll's head or quickly and carefully dip the doll under water and talk about baptism by full immersion. Ask your godchild to help you read and discuss parts of the baptismal service.

⩘ Prayers of Thanksgiving over Water

Read to (or with) your godchild the prayer said to bless
the water used in baptism:

> We thank you, Almighty God, for the gift of water. Over
> it the Holy Spirit moved in the beginning of creation.
> Through it you led the children of Israel out of their
> bondage in Egypt into the land of promise. In it your Son
> Jesus received the baptism of John and was anointed by the
> Holy Spirit as the Messiah, the Christ, to lead us, through
> his death and resurrection, from the bondage of sin into
> everlasting life.
>
> We thank you, Father, for the water of Baptism. In it
> we are buried with Christ in his death. By it we share in his
> resurrection. Through it we are reborn by the Holy Spirit.
> Therefore in joyful obedience to your Son, we bring into
> his fellowship those who come to him in faith, baptizing
> them in the Name of the Father, and of the Son, and of the
> Holy Spirit.
>
> Now sanctify this water, we pray you, by the power of
> your Holy Spirit, that those who here are cleansed from sin
> and born again may continue for ever in the risen life of
> Jesus Christ our Savior. To him, to you, and to the Holy
> Spirit, be all honor and glory, now and for ever. *Amen.*
> (BCP, 306–7)

Chapter 5

"Once upon a Time"

Sharing God's Story
with Your Godchild

"Will you proclaim by word and example
the Good News of God in Christ?"

Stories are one of the most important ways in which we communicate. They are treasure chests that contain much of what human beings hold to be important: our values, history, ideas, heroes, and our most important thoughts about life. In ancient cultures, people told stories as a way of creating and nurturing group identity; a way to define who they were and how they differed from other peoples they encountered. This shared folklore held hints about the tribe's identity and what they held as sacred. It gave accounts of important battles and helped illustrate the values of the group. When people told stories, they were passing on their history to the next generation of tribal members who were learning both where they came from and who they had the potential to become.

And still today, everybody loves a story. When we share quality stories with our children, we pass on the best of what humanity has to offer. We share the gifts of faith, hope, courage, and sacrifice. We teach our children what love looks like and how to live as people who believe in grace and resurrection.

There are many wonderful stories you can share with your godchild. And as you tell these stories to the next generation, you continue the ancient tradition of our ancestors. As you share the story of God and God's people, you pass on the good news of our sacred tribe.

Sharing God's Words

God helps Moses speak to Pharaoh	Exodus 4:10–12
Tell God's story to your children	Deuteronomy 6:5–9
Teaching children about God	Psalm 34
Proclaiming God's story	Psalm 71:17
"Good news refreshes the body"	Proverbs 15:30
Good news for the oppressed	Isaiah 61:1
"As you go, proclaim the good news . . ."	Matthew 10:7
Proclaim to all creation	Mark 16:15
Faith formed by mother and grandmother	2 Timothy 1:1–5
Chosen and holy, in order to proclaim	1 Peter 2:9

Sometimes we worry that we do not have enough theological expertise or Bible knowledge to adequately share God's Story. This can feel like a daunting job if we do not remind ourselves that the Story of God is continuously echoed in our own personal stories. Relax and trust the ways in which God has been revealed to you. You do not have to know all the stories of the Bible and their meaning in order to share the evidence of God's Story in your life.

Pointing out God's presence in everyday life can be an ongoing conversation with your godchild that helps her discover sacred spaces in her own life. When you spend time with your godchild, watch for ways to call her attention to God's presence in the world around us—a new puppy in the neighborhood, a glorious sunset, the vivid fall leaves you see on a walk, the way that families love each other and practice forgiveness on a daily basis. All of these ordinary things are reminders of our loving Creator who teaches us how to love.

Another important way we learn about God is by hearing and telling God's stories. Reading and telling Bible stories to your godchild helps her see where God's Story intersects with her own story. As we tell and retell the ancient stories of Moses, Abraham, Ruth, David, Mary, Jesus, and the apostles, we also teach what it looks like when God calls our name and invites us to come and follow.

Sharing the Good News of God with the next generation is an honor. Being a godparent is very much like being a trusted tribal elder. It is your job to help this child know who we are and where we come from, to share the secrets of our tribe and offer glimpses of the sacred. So go and tell the Story . . .

Ernesto's Story: Telling the Stories

Thomas and Stephen stayed at our house for awhile, and stories played an important role in our time together. Not only did they tell stories of their previous family adventures, but they shared their prayerful hopes for love-filled future lives. We also had a ritual story time before bed. I read books to them that I knew would hold great meaning for them past, present, and future. Some of their favorites were The Boxcar Children by Gertrude Chandler Warner, A Wrinkle in Time by Madeleine L'Engle, and The Lion, the Witch, and the Wardrobe by C. S. Lewis. After each chapter there was often discussion of how these stories related to their own experiences.

But they got most excited when they would hear their names in the Scripture readings in church on Sunday, or on their patron saint's feast day. And since we attended St. Stephen's Episcopal Church, Stephen felt that it was "his" church. On the drive home we would talk about the story they heard and what their saint was like. At home we'd pull out the Bible and look carefully at the reading, taking time for more detailed questions and reflections on what they might do in the same circumstances. This Bible search was quite fun and often we would have to look up saint stories for the other children around that day so they wouldn't feel left out.

Explore the lives of the saints with your godchild. Consider a children's version of the lives of the saints for story time or as a gift. (See *www.godparenting.info* for suggestions.) It would be beneficial for your godchild to have, or choose, a patron saint to look up to.

≷ Sharing God's Good News

Bible stories cover basic truths, so find a children's Bible you like and set a solid foundation by starting to read to your godchild when they are very young. It is surprising how early children can be caught up in stories. I (Nancy) remember trying to nurse my youngest son and read to my toddler at the same time, but the little guy was often less interested in dinner than he was in the book.

As your godchild grows, you will want to explore biblical stories in greater depth. Find and share an illustrated book of the biblical customs and archeology, such as *If You'd Been There in Bible Times* by Stephanie Jeffs or *The Complete Bible Handbook* by John Bowker. Libraries often have great resources that you and your godchild can explore together, or see *www.godparenting.info* for more ideas.

Bible stories also come alive when viewing videos with biblical themes. Discuss with older godchildren how the movie director and actors add their own interpretation in their portrayals of the written word. One notable example is *The Visual Bible*'s version of Matthew in which Jesus appears as joyous and full of life.

As you and your godchild develop a shared library of biblical accounts, you will be able to relate applications of these stories to everyday life. For instance, in today's mobile society, many children move either across town or across the country, but did you ever stop to realize how

Choosing a Children's Bible

⌇ For young children, pick something with bright, color-ful illustrations and large print, such as The Beginner's Bible by Karyn Henley or Tomie DePaola's Book of Bible Stories. Older children will be drawn to lavish illustrations, such as Words of Gold illustrated by Lois Rock or The Bible for Children by Murray Watts, illustrated by Helen Cann.

⌇ Look for options that spark a child's imagination. Try Does God Have a Big Toe? by Rabbi Marc Gellman— a hilarious and heartwarming collection of midrash, the Jewish tradition of telling stories about Bible passages— or The Family Story Bible by Ralph Milton.

⌇ Be careful to avoid language that could be interpreted as anti-Semitic. Watch for phrases like "the Jews" (implying all Jews for all time) especially in the passion narratives. The Children's Bible in 365 Stories by Mary Batchelor was commended by the American Interfaith Institute for modifications that pay particular attention to this issue.

⌇ Older children may enjoy reading Marked! by Steve Ross, a graphic novel that tells the story of the Gospel of Mark in comic-book style. This edgy depiction of the gospel is framed in a modern context, but solidly connected with Scripture.

Choosing a Children's Bible (continued)

≷ One final caveat: Check theology carefully. There are
several children's Bibles that retell the story of Eden
using "Satan" instead of a snake or that skip the events
of Holy Week and the crucifixion altogether. Also,
watch for the tendency of some versions to moralize
and/or over-interpret difficult Scripture passages. If you
need help, or are not sure about a particular version,
talk with your clergy or Christian educator.

many stories in the Bible are about moving? Consider:
Abraham and Sarah and the promised land; Joseph, and
later his family, moving to Egypt; Moses and the Israelites
leaving Egypt; Ruth following her mother-in-law to a
strange town; the Hebrew exiles; Jesus moving from city
to city (especially good is the Emmaus trip); and the
various journeys of the apostles. If your godchild's family
decides to move, assure her that God will be with her, and
help her consider what God might be calling her to do in
her new environment.

Imagine with your godchild what it might be like if
some of the biblical characters were involved in family,
local, or national events. When you eat together, remember the stories of the loaves and fishes or the meals
Jesus shared with the disciples. You can also discuss what
Jesus or one of the prophets might have to say about a

current political debate. When your godchild is facing new or puzzling situations, ask her to picture herself interacting with biblical characters. Look for biblical accounts that seem similar or ask, "What would the prophets say?" or "What would Jesus do in a similar situation?" (A biblical concordance can be a helpful tool to locate a Scripture passage when you only remember a word or phrase.) When you know the stories of the Bible, you can help your godchild listen to the advice of these ancient characters.

Remember that the story of God interacting with God's people is still continuing today. The Bible is not only for use at church. When you and your godchild play church at home or break bread together at meals, remember to proclaim God's words. Talk about how certain Scriptures might be helpful to understanding a current situation and ask her to think about how God speaks to us through the Bible. Ask your godchild what she would say if she had to offer a sermon on this topic. What might we do differently because of God's message of love? How can we proclaim God's good news by example?

As your godchild gets older, explore different types of writing in the Bible: Many of the books in the Old Testament (also called the Hebrew Scriptures) contain the history of early tribes and their laws; the Psalms are ancient poems and songs; the Gospels are accounts of Jesus' life, death, and resurrection; the book of Acts records the activities of the early church; and Epistles are letters written to encourage early Christians. Once you

Storytelling Methods

There are hundreds of ways to tell God's stories—reading from the Bible is just one of them. Here are some other ideas:

- ≩ Read and then retell the story in your own words.
- ≩ Use dolls or figures to portray the story—keep a child-friendly nativity set (wood, fabric, etc.) out all year.
- ≩ Act out the parts, trying on different characters.
- ≩ Imagine what happens before, after, or "between the words" in well-known Bible stories.
- ≩ With teenagers, read and discuss biblical fiction, such as The Red Tent by Anita Diamant or I Came to Love You Late by Joyce Landorf.
- ≩ Sing hymns or songs that portray the stories or better yet, make up your own.
- ≩ Draw pictures or comic strips to illustrate the story.
- ≩ Play charades—one person silently acts out clues while the other person tries to guess the story.
- ≩ Make simple puppets—using socks or plain paper lunchbags—and have the puppets tell the story.

discuss the different types of literature found in the Bible, you and your godchild can work together to prayerfully write your own history, laws, poems, songs, good news, letters, and acts.

As a godparent you may wish to deepen your own knowledge and appreciation of Scripture. Perhaps you would like to join a Bible study or set aside time for personal reading. You might also consider becoming a lector or reader at your church. This would allow you to regularly study, pray over, and proclaim various biblical readings.

Bible Stories and Where to Find Them

Old Testament

Creation story	Genesis 1; 2
Adam and Eve are tempted	Genesis 3:1–24
Noah and the ark	Genesis 6:1–9:28
God's covenant with Abraham	Genesis 15:1–21
Jacob's ladder dream	Genesis 28:10–22
Joseph and his brothers	Genesis 37:1–36
Moses and Pharaoh	Exodus 5:1–7:13
The Ten Commandments	Exodus 20:1–21
Samson and Delilah	Judges 13:1–16:31
Ruth and Naomi	Ruth 1:1–4:22
The calling of Samuel	1 Samuel 3:1–4:1
David and Goliath	1 Samuel 17:1–58
Elijah and Elisha	1 Kings 19:19–21
Queen Esther	Esther 1–10

Bible Stories and Where to Find Them (continued)

New Testament

The birth of Jesus	Luke 2:1–20
Boy Jesus in the temple	Luke 2:41–52
Jesus' baptism	Matthew 3:13–17
The calling of the Twelve	Mark 3:13–19; John 1:35–51
The Good Samaritan	Luke 10:25–37
The Prodigal Son	Luke 15:11–32
Feeding of 5000	John 6:3–13
Sermon on the Mount	Matthew 5:1–7:29; Luke 6:17–49
The Passion	Luke 22:1–23:56
The Resurrection	John 20:1–18
The early church	Acts 2
The calling of Paul	Acts 9:1–31
Paul's first missionary journey	Acts 13:1–14:28

⋛ The Line between Sacred and Secular

"Books on all subjects . . . can stir children's hearts, widen their imaginations, and break down some of the barriers our culture has built between sacred and secular."

—*Gretchen Wolff Pritchard*

Bible stories are not the only stories that hold echoes of the Holy One. There are many storybooks that teach God's truths even when God is not mentioned by name. Children's books are one of my (Tracey's) great passions and I have spent many years collecting them. Here are some of my favorites, and there are more on our website *www.godparenting.info*:

Finding God in Children's Books

Great books about reconciliation and compromise; enchanting for all ages.

⋛ A Small Miracle by Peter Collington—my favorite Christmas book. A wonderfully wordless magical story about a nativity scene that comes to life.

⋛ God Bless the Gargoyles by Dav Pilkey—when gargoyles hear people call them ugly, angels rush in to bless and befriend them, scattering "songs of rebirth" upon all who wrestle with loneliness or grief.

Finding God in Children's Books (continued)

≷ God's Paintbrush by Sandy Eisenberg Sasso—a comforting book about all the ways God's presence can be found in the world around us, written by a Jewish rabbi and mother. Includes questions to discuss with your child.

≷ Old Turtle and Old Turtle and the Broken Truth by Douglas Wood—how all the animals of the earth see God and how Old Turtle stops them from arguing.

≷ Psalm Twenty-Three illustrated by Tim Ladwig—the original text of Psalm 23 poignantly illustrated using a modern African American family in an urban environment.

≷ The Empty Pot by Demi—a magnificent story about a little boy in China named Ping and the importance of doing your best, regardless of the outcome.

≷ The Quiltmaker's Gift by Jeff Brumbeau—a magical quiltmaker refuses to make one of her phenomenal quilts for a greedy king until he gives away some of his countless possessions.

≷ The Runaway Bunny by Margaret Wise Brown—the well-loved tale of a loving parent who will go to any extreme to reassure her child. Great example of how God loves us.

This list contains just a few short suggestions to get you started. Add your own favorites and look for even more stories to share with your godchild. Whether you read the stories or retell them from your imagination, whether you share Bible stories or other great stories that reflect God's timeless truths, sharing stories with your godchild is an important thing to do. Stories help us understand ourselves and can give us insight into other people or even help us comprehend God. As we share stories and experiment with different story lines, we are learning how to love and how to live. Even more than that, we are learning how to be transformed.

Chapter 6

"Ouch! I'll Bet That Hurt!"

Loving Your Neighbor

"Will you seek and serve Christ in all persons, loving your neighbor as yourself?"

Baptism welcomes us into the family of God and makes us witnesses to God's love. First we are *welcomed*, and then, after experiencing God's love firsthand, we are *witnesses*. The baptismal covenant affirms both these roles. The first several questions in the covenant are about internal commitments: Do you believe in God the Father, Son, and Holy Spirit? Will you continue in the apostles' teaching and fellowship, in the breaking of bread and in the prayers? Will you persevere in resisting evil? But then the questions turn to focus on our external interactions with the world: Will you proclaim the Good News of God in Christ? Will you seek and serve Christ in all persons, loving your neighbor as yourself? (See BCP 304–5.)

This is a tall order—first trying to see Christ in all persons, then trying to serve the Christ in all persons, remembering to care for others with the same life-affirming tenacity in which we care for ourselves. God never says we should love only those with whom our lives are intimately intertwined. Instead, we are given a more difficult task: Over and over again, the words of Scripture call us to remember the stranger, protect the foreigner, care for the widow and the orphan. This fourth promise in our baptismal covenant reminds us that *every* human being has the potential to reveal Christ to us. We are to care for *every* human being with the same tender care we would use to care for Jesus himself. The enormity of this task can seem overwhelming.

We live in a world where every community has needs and problems. But in spite of this and even after centuries of talking about our desire to be more unified, we divide ourselves from one another in so many ways. We're not content just to divide ourselves by the big things—by race, by class, by religion. We look for even more ways to define "who's in and who's out"—by gender or sexual orientation, by political party, or just by differing opinions. As a godparent, you can help your godchild understand that God's kingdom is never about being divided into exclusive groups, but rather about being inclusively embraced in God's love for all.

You can help your godchild understand that sometimes even churches get it wrong—we focus on the wrong things, we hold grudges, we allow our communities to be torn apart by disagreements, and we fight among ourselves instead of focusing on God's love for the world just outside our lovely stained glass windows—a world that desperately needs to hear the Good News of God in Christ. But with God's help and your guidance, your godchild can learn to help to create a church that is growing and moving in the right direction—a church that recognizes Christ in all persons.

Serving God Globally

To get a sense of how much work there is to do, consider these statistics and information adapted with permission from the website of Episcopalians for Global Reconciliation:

One *billion* people (approximately one sixth of the people on the planet) live on less than $1.00 a day. Every day 30,000 children die from *preventable* consequences of extreme poverty—that's one every three seconds. Every year 500,000 women die from complications of pregnancy—most of them exacerbated by poverty.

In the year 2000, at the dawning of a new millennium, leaders from 189 nations—including the United States—agreed to cut extreme global poverty in half by 2015. These world leaders unanimously adopted the Millennium Declaration which led to eight specific Millennium Development Goals (MDGs), to be achieved by 2015:

1. Eradicate extreme poverty and hunger.
2. Achieve universal primary education.
3. Promote gender equality and empower women.
4. Reduce child mortality.
5. Improve maternal health.
6. Combat HIV/AIDS, malaria, and other diseases.
7. Ensure environmental sustainability.
8. Create a global partnership for development.

If the world meets the Millennium Development Goals, more than 500 million people would be lifted out of extreme poverty; more than 300 million people would no longer be hungry. Sound too good to be true? Experts believe these goals are attainable with the resources we *already* have at our disposal.

There are many ways to help our world reach the Millennium Development Goals. Start by helping your godchild become aware of the issues. For instance, ask him to consider how "$1.00 a day" compares with his allowance or how much money his family spends in an average day. For more information about the MDGs or about how to get involved, check out the websites of the United Nations (*www.un.org/millenniumgoals*) and Episcopalians for Global Reconciliation (*www.e4gr.org*).

There are many ways to help our world reach the Millennium Development Goals. Start by helping your godchild become aware of the issues. For instance, ask him to consider how "$1.00 a day" compares with his allowance, or how much money his family spends in an average day. For more information about this program or about how to get involved, check out the websites of the United Nations (*www.un.org/millenniumgoals*) and Episcopalians for Global Reconciliation (*www.e4gr.org*).

Just as all Christians form the body of Christ, all people of the world are made in God's image and are invited to be members of God's kingdom. But in order to be a healthy, functioning kingdom, each member needs to recognize and respect God's image in each other. The overall vision here is not charity work, but recognizing that each person has a role to play and a contribution to make. Offering help to an individual member of the body is a way of working together as we watch in expectation for a day when all people are healthy and contributing members of God's kingdom. The following prayer attributed to St. Francis is a great one to share with your godchild:

> Lord, make us instruments of your peace.
> Where there is hatred, let us sow love;
> where there is injury, pardon;
> where there is discord, union;
> where there is doubt, faith;
> where there is despair, hope;
> where there is darkness, light;
> where there is sadness, joy.
> Grant that we may not so much seek to be consoled
>   as to console;
> to be understood as to understand;
> to be loved as to love.
> For it is in giving that we receive;
> it is in pardoning that we are pardoned;
> and it is in dying that we are born to eternal life. *Amen.*
>   (BCP, 833)

⚡ Serving God Individually

Being part of a global effort is important and admirable, but seeking and serving Christ in all persons does not have to happen on a big scale to be valid and important. You and your godchild can start by simply looking to the people who share your homes or neighborhoods. A first step to living more fully into our baptismal promise is to pray that God will give us eyes to really *see* the face of Christ in people we encounter. We can commit to seek out people who are different from us and get to know them. We can remember to treat each other in the ways we would wish to be treated. We can remind ourselves and our godchildren that all human beings—even those with whom we vehemently disagree—are beloved children of God who have been made in the image of the Creator.

In the Hindi and Nepali cultures, the greeting "*Namaste*" can be translated as "the Divine in me recognizes the Divine in you," or "I greet the place where you and I are one." In Christianity, we have the words of Jesus (commonly referred to as "the golden rule") "Do unto others as you would have them do unto you, for this is the law and the prophets" (see Matt 7:12). These words are echoed again in Luke when a man who knows the laws of Moses approaches Jesus and asks, "Teacher, what must I do to inherit eternal life?" Jesus returns the question by asking, "What is written in the law? What do you read there?" The man promptly responds with the expected answer, "You shall love the Lord your God with all your heart, and with all your soul, and with all your strength, and with all your mind; and love your neighbor as yourself." When Jesus assures the man he has given the proper response, the man pushes Jesus a bit further by asking, "And who is my neighbor?"

Jesus replies by telling the now well-known story of the Good Samaritan: A man is traveling the steep, dangerous road that winds from Jerusalem down to Jericho

Godparenting

when he is attacked by robbers and left for dead. The man is passed, first by a priest—an upper-class leader in society who wishes to remain ritually clean, and then by a Levite—a descendant of Levi whose role it was to assist in the temple. But then along comes a Samaritan—a man thought to be of a socially inferior mixed race. The Samaritan risks defilement and further exclusion and helps the wounded man, not only tending his wounds, but also taking him to an inn where he can recover. After telling the story, Jesus volleys these challenging words back to the lawyer, "Which of these three proved to be the neighbor?" and the man replies, "The one who showed mercy." Jesus responds with a simple, direct command: "Go and do likewise." (See Luke 10:25–37.)

Jesus makes it clear that our neighbors are not always who we think they are and that the mandates of Love are stronger than the letter of the Law. These are important principles to put into practice in our own lives today. In whatever ways we can first learn and then teach our godchildren to show mercy to other people or to recognize others as reflections of God's image, we have made progress in fulfilling our baptismal vows.

⧢ Caring and Connectedness

In the Episcopal worship service, we conclude our Holy Eucharist with one of two post-communion prayers, both of which talk about the importance of serving:

"Send us now into the world in peace, and grant us strength and courage to love and serve you with gladness and singleness of heart. . . ." (BCP, 365)

"And now, Father, send us out to do the work you have given us to do, to love and serve you as faithful witnesses of Christ our Lord. . . ." (BCP, 366)

In addition, our services are often dismissed with the words:

"Go in peace to love and serve the Lord. Thanks be to God." (BCP, 366)

Long before your godchild is able to communicate with you, he will have heard these words about the importance of service many, many times. Part of your responsibility as a godparent is to help him understand and experience how we are connected to other people and why helping other people is important. In his wonderful book *The Way of the Wolf*, Martin Bell tells the story of a little boy named Thajir who learns secrets of life from the wind, including this bit of wisdom about human connectedness:

You are everyone who ever was and everyone who will ever be. You are the whole of creation—past, present, and future. Decisions that you make today, in what is called the here and now, will validate or invalidate everything that has gone before, and make possible or impossible everything that is to come. Anything that hurts anyone, hurts you. Anything that helps anyone, helps you. It is not possible to gain from another's loss or to lose from another's gain. Your life is immensely important. Everything depends on you.

When we teach our children the importance of caring for people, we reinforce the idea that human beings are connected to each other because we are all children of God. You can help your godchild understand this by talking about the people whose lives are linked to yours. As you help your godchild see the elaborate chains of connection we have throughout our schools, churches, and communities, you are helping to make "seeking and serving Christ in all persons" a natural part of your godchild's spiritual development.

Finding God in Service

≷ When possible make special Sunday dates to attend church with your godchild and afterward do some ministry of service together.

≷ Talk about the needs in your city. Do you see homeless people on the street? Do you know of agencies that help people who don't have enough food? Is there a food bank or homeless shelter where you and your godchild can volunteer together?

≷ Visit people who are sick or homebound. Bring a meal, or pictures you have colored with your godchild, or a

Finding God in Service (continued)

potted plant you have picked out together. Share in-home communion if it is offered by your church.

≋ Volunteer at an animal shelter to help clean or walk the animals.

≋ Visit www.habitat.org to find information about Habitat for Humanity and how children can help.

≋ Help your godchild gather coats, clothes, toys, books, canned food, or other items to donate to others.

≋ Children are great sharers. Teach your godchild how God shares with us and how everything we have ultimately comes from God. Help your godchild develop the habit of setting aside at least ten percent to give back to God's kingdom by selecting service projects to support with time and money.

≋ Deuteronomy 14:22–26 is an interesting passage about sharing a tenth of your possessions with God. It also describes a pilgrimage. Read the passage with your godchild and discuss what this means and how you might be able to accomplish this.

≋ Talk about poverty here in our country and around the world. A wonderful book to help your godchild gain some perspective of global numbers is If the World Were a Village by David J. Smith. This book boils statistics down to a village of 100 people—where 9 people would speak English, only 24 people would have television, and 17 of them would be unable to read.

※ Look for ways you and your godchild can build bridges with someone who represents diversity for you. Visit with people who are from different countries, practice different religions, speak different languages, or are different in some other way. After your visits, talk about how each person may have seemed different from you and how each seemed similar.

※ A great book to help children understand a broader sense of humanity is Whoever You Are by Mem Fox. We may have different skin colors, languages, environment, and lifestyles, but we love and laugh, hurt and cry in the same way.

Lezlie's Story: Caring for Others

We have two little girls, ages six and eight. It's really important to me that we are honest and direct with our children about all aspects of life, not just the easy, happy stuff. My kids are very privileged, and while I don't want to burden my children with a lot of guilt, I also want them to realize that not everyone is lucky enough to live the way that we do. We talk about how human beings can help each other—how sometimes you are the one giving help and sometimes you are the one receiving help—and how both parts are important. When we are in a position to help someone else, I've discovered that my daughters feel more personally involved when we find projects that specifically affect children, instead of just talking hypothetically about "people" who don't have enough food to eat or warm clothes to wear.

At least once a year, we go through our overflowing closets and gather up clothes, games, or toys to donate to charity. Rather than boxing up the items myself, I encourage the girls to identify some personal belongings they are willing to give away. It's a natural human tendency to want to hold on to things, so sometimes it is a difficult process when we come across something we haven't used in a long time but are not sure we are ready to part with. I try to gently explain that there are other six- and eight-year-old children in our city who may not have a single toy to play with, and perhaps this object that was once such a cherished part of our daily lives might be the absolutely perfect thing to give to another child who needs something special to love.

Another project our family really enjoys is our elementary school's relationship with a "buddy school." The buddy school is located in an area of town where 80 percent of the children are on a free or reduced-cost lunch program, and parents have few resources to share with the school. Our school organizes drives for school supplies and books during the year, and then in December, each family in our school is encouraged to adopt a buddy school family for Christmas. We are given a sheet of paper that anonymously describes the family—how many children, how many adults, what their ages and sizes are, and what they would like to receive for Christmas—both gifts they want and gifts they need. When our family goes to buy the presents, we point out how some things we might just assume they have—hats, gloves, scarves—are the very things this child most needs. Talking about specific examples seems to really help our children understand how other people live, and I believe this awareness helps make them more compassionate toward others.

I want to reinforce these lessons, not just by taking on special projects, but also as part of our everyday life. Our next-door neighbors have little girls the same ages as my daughters, and the four girls have been close playmates and friends. The family is from Egypt, and last year when they had a baby, the new mother was really missing her sisters and friends back home who would have loved to come take care of her, so we offered to provide a week of dinners. My girls love to cook and are great at chopping and mixing. Even when parts of the meal preparation were too difficult for them, they stayed in the kitchen, talking or drawing cards and pictures to accompany our meals. It was fun to make the meal together each evening and then have the girls walk over with us to deliver the dinner next door.

I'm proud of my family and the things we have accomplished, and I am proud of my daughters who are loving and considerate, and who are learning that there are things we can do to continually help make the world a better place for all of us to live.

⚡ The Power of Oil

Oil is an ancient symbol of healing and protection. With infants we use baby oil to protect and guard their skin. In massage therapy, oil is used to ease friction and care for the body. Oil soaks in, softening you, becoming part of you, allowing healing to begin. Oil has been used to keep infection away—oil protects you, sealing against things that could bring you harm. These basic uses of oil, in themselves, have many implications for you and your godchild for service and ministry in God's name. All throughout history, however, oil has also been used for special occasions. It has been used to mark people and things as special or sacred.

In the Hebrew Scriptures we see many stories of people anointed with oil to symbolize a special calling—especially prophets, priests, and kings. The oil was a symbol of God's Spirit that would help in this new role or ministry. The anointing of David as king by the prophet Samuel says it well: "Then Samuel took the horn of oil, and anointed him in the presence of his brothers; and the spirit of the LORD came mightily upon David from that day forward" (1 Sam 16:13).

Jesus followed this tradition, and in fact, the Hebrew word *Messiah* means "anointed one." Jesus' followers recognized and proclaimed him as Messiah, and the early church understood that his role was as a king and priest but also included elements of servanthood. The word

Messiah was translated into Greek as "Christ." Jesus Christ was anointed to do God's work in the world, and therefore those who follow Christ, "Christians," are *also* anointed through baptism to receive the Holy Spirit and be in partnership with God.

Special oil called "chrism" is set aside for anointing each new Christian in baptism. The chrism has been blessed by the bishop with this prayer: "Eternal Father, whose blessed Son was anointed by the Holy Spirit to be the Savior and servant of all, we pray you to consecrate this oil, that those who are sealed with it may share in the royal priesthood of Jesus Christ; who lives and reigns with you and the Holy Spirit, for ever and ever. *Amen*" (BCP, 307). During the service of Holy Baptism, the celebrant uses the oil of chrism to mark the sign of a cross on your godchild's forehead saying, "You are sealed by the Holy Spirit in Baptism and marked as Christ's own for ever" (BCP, 308). The oil of anointing reminds us that we are both inheritors and servants of the kingdom of God *and* part of the royal priesthood. This special role is echoed when the whole congregation welcomes the newly baptized immediately following the anointing: "We receive you into the household of God. Confess the faith of Christ crucified, proclaim his resurrection, and share with us in his eternal priesthood" (BCP, 308).

Seeking and serving Christ in all persons clearly indicates the Christian's role as loving servant, and oil is an excellent symbol of this aspect of our baptismal covenant.

As a godparent, you take on a special servant role of helping your godchild, but all Christians are called to be servants of God and that is a role to be proud of and to celebrate. You may want to honor this tradition with your godchild in a formal way by doing your own anointing or blessing, perhaps before undertaking a special service project. You can use olive or sweet almond oil, or you can create a mixture like the Hebrew anointing oil, which was a unique blend of oil with special spices (see Exod 30:22–33).

Before your anointing ceremony, discuss with your godchild the importance of the service that you are about to perform, how it fits in with the broader kingdom of God, and your role as servants of God. Then share the gospel account of how Jesus sent out the disciples two by two (see Luke 10:1–9). You can formalize your acceptance of the role as loving servants with a prayer, either one that you compose together or this one adapted from the Episcopal Consecration of the Deacon (deacon means "servant").

> Make us, O Lord, modest and humble, strong and constant, to observe the discipline of Christ. Let our lives and teaching so reflect your commandments, that through us many may come to know you and love you. As your Son came not to be served but to serve, may we share in Christ's service, and come to the unending glory of him who, with you and the Holy Spirit, lives and reigns, one God, for ever and ever. Amen. (BCP, 545)

Finally, use the oil to take turns marking a sign of the cross on each other's foreheads saying something like, "Receive this oil as a sign of your authority to serve in God's kingdom." Alternatively, you can anoint each other's hands, marking a cross in each palm saying, "May the work you do bring honor to God and blessing to others."

God's Words about Oil

Oil used to commemorate holy place	Genesis 28:10–22
Oil contributed to make sanctuary	Exodus 25:1–9
Priests ordained using anointing oil	Exodus 29:1–9
Recipe for sacred anointing oil	Exodus 30:22–33
Ritual cleansing of temple with oil	Leviticus 14:10–20
Oil as tithe offering	Deuteronomy 12:17
Saul anointed first king with oil	1 Samuel 10:1
Widow's unending supply of oil	1 Kings 17:8–16
Esther's beauty oil treatments	Esther 2:12
Oil as a part of grooming	Matthew 6:17

God's Words about Oil (continued)

Be ready with oil in your lamps	Matthew 25:1–13
Jesus' feet anointed with oil	Luke 7:36–50
Oil used as first aid by Good Samaritan	Luke 10:34
Healing oil used for the sick	James 5:14
Anointments used for burial	Luke 23:52–24:3

≋ Sharing

From a very young age, children are taught the importance of sharing. Learning to share toys or the attention of a parent is important, but there are also lessons of sharing in things related to God and church. We share in our responsibility to be God's partners and take care of Creation. We share meals together, and we share the bread and wine of communion. We share our lives with other people in our families and communities. We try to stay aware of global issues and do all we can to bring about a God-like kingdom where resources are shared and everyone has enough. Sharing is important because it teaches us both to give *and* receive. I (Nancy) remember my sons always wanted to share my ice-cream cone, but they also wanted and needed me to accept whatever they offered to me. By accepting their gifts I showed that I respected them and valued their contribution to our relationship.

Robert's Story: Learning to Share

As a priest, one of my favorite things to do is distribute communion. One Sunday morning, I was distributing bread, which on this particular Sunday was actually a thin cracker-like wafer. As I moved down the altar rail, I reached a young toddler whose hand was held out to receive. I placed the wafer in his hand and said, "The Body of Christ."

Immediately, the little boy held out his other hand, in which he was holding a cracker he had been nibbling on. He placed his cracker in my hand and said back to me, "The Body of Christ." I took a small bite of his cracker and then handed it back to the little fellow and was rewarded with a brilliant smile.

After church, the boy's mother came through the receiving line and told me that her son was just a little over a year old. She also told me she hadn't yet heard him talk. In other words, if these weren't actually the boy's first words, they were at least his first sentence.

Never again would I wonder about why we share communion with young children. Yes, the boy was mimicking what he saw, but even then he showed a level of understanding that far exceeded his age. He understood at communion we are all equal: The priest may be the one presiding, but we all give and receive. He understood he is welcome here, just as he is, with the knowledge and the gifts he has right now, limited though they may seem. Most of all, he learns that communion is about sharing: Jesus sharing with us and us sharing with each other.

Sharing bread as a god-family can become rich in meaning. In the Polish home I (Nancy) grew up in, we celebrated the Christmas tradition of *Oplatek* (also referred to as angel bread or the bread of love). This is wafer-thin bread with images of Jesus, Mary, and Joseph, angels, stars, shepherds, and kings. During the main holiday meal it was brought out around the extended family table. Traditionally, it would start with the youngest breaking off a piece of the bread offered by the oldest person, followed with a joyous Christmas greeting. Each would then share his piece with another person until everyone had shared with everyone else. *Oplatek* is still available in some Polish churches and on the web, but you and your godchild can start this type of tradition with any type of bread. The aim is sharing, reconciliation, and reunion with all members. It was through this tradition outside church services that I came to a greater awareness of Christ's presence in all. We are connected through the incarnation celebrated at Christmas and realize this by sharing bread as equals in the Body of Christ.

Chapter 7

"That's Not Fair!"

God's Justice and Peace

"Will you strive for justice and peace among all people,
and respect the dignity of every human being?"

Children want things to be fair. They want to have choices, have a say in things, and feel as if they have some control over their own lives. They want to be able to use their voices and have their words make a difference. Of course, all those things are true for adults too, but somehow as we get older, we often lose our sense of indignation about what's fair and what's not, and we are less likely to make noise about the injustices of life. Your job as a godparent is to help ensure that the same godchild who is quick to shout, "That's not fair!" about losing a board game or having to go to bed at a certain time does not grow up to be an adult who sees a world full of true discrimination and inequity but remains silent. The prophet Isaiah warns against complacency but promises that when God's Spirit is poured upon us, "Then justice will dwell in the wilderness, and righteousness abide in the fruitful field. The effect of righteousness will be peace, and the result of righteousness, quietness and trust forever" (Isa 32:16–17).

Being a Christian means many different things: It means working on your relationship with God and learning how to pray. It means trying to understand the apostles' teaching or the words of Scripture. It means belonging to a Christian community and using your gifts as a member of the Body of Christ. It means lots of different things to lots of different people, but if our Christianity is only directed inward toward ourselves and upward toward God, we are missing a primary aspect of Christianity, one that we see in the example of Christ—reaching outward to other people. One of the hallmarks of Christ's ministry was that he consistently reached out to others. Caring for people is a basic tenet of faith, and even before the birth of Jesus, we hear the words of the Old Testament echoing a consistent message of a faith that includes connection and relationship with other people. In the book of Micah, we find a brief but meaningful summary of the requirements of genuine faith: "What does the Lord require of you but to do justice, and to love kindness, and to walk humbly with your God?" (Mic 6:8).

Learning to strive for justice, work for peace, and respect the dignity of every human being are fairly easy concepts to understand, but incredibly difficult to consistently put into practice. However, learning to incorporate these beliefs into our daily lives is the real crux of Christianity. More than twenty-five years ago, my (Tracey's) youth minister offered me this piece of wisdom that has become my personal touchstone: "We practice daily what we *truly* believe—the rest is just religious babble." The thinking part of me often wants to debate these words, to say that it's too simplistic to try to boil a complex, growing faith into a single statement, and yet these words remain in my head and in my heart, challenging me to put my faith into action. When I shift into my "head only" mode, these words prick at my conscience, pushing me to walk out into the world and *do* something to make my life count for more than just so much religious babble.

Jesus modeled authentic faith for us—he lived what he believed. He was an advocate for the poor, the oppressed, the outcast, the ones who have no voice. He interacted regularly with unexpected people on the fringes of society and routinely broke bread with people outside the accepted boundaries. From his very first sermon, Jesus makes it clear what his ministry is about as he reads from Isaiah: "The Spirit of the Lord is upon me, because he has anointed me to bring good news to the poor. He has sent me to proclaim release to the captives and recovery of sight to the blind, to let the oppressed go free. . . ." (Luke 4:16–21). When I (Tracey) dig through all the sermons I've listened to or offered, all the books I've read, all the religious thoughts I've had, at the end of the day, this is who I think I'm called to be: an advocate for the poor, the oppressed, the outcast, the ones who have no voice.

Baptism is not just a special day, or a simple a rite of passage we can fondly remember with pictures in a scrapbook, or elaborate white heirloom gowns, or parties where families gather together and celebrate. Baptism is a radical call to a lifetime of ministry and service, a commitment to work tirelessly for justice, to seek and cultivate true peace in our lives and in our world, and to "make no peace with oppression" (BCP, 260). It is an invitation to live in a brand new kingdom—the kingdom of God.

≷ Living Our Vows

Living as a baptized Christian isn't always easy. You and your godchild decide to be Christians, not just on important days like baptism or confirmation, but each and every day, you choose again to live a life that demonstrates your choice. Being a Christian involves serious decisions that may lead to real sacrifices. Jesus was crucified as a result of the life he led, the beliefs he held, and the decisions he made. While none of us today are going to face crucifixion, there are times we risk giving up things that are important to us in order to be followers of Christ. When other people look at your life, do they see something different about you? Or, as it has been said, "If you were put on trial for being a Christian, would there be enough evidence to convict you?" When the inevitable opportunities arise, can you talk about your relationship with God without fear or embarrassment? Are you comfortable defining yourself as part of God's kingdom? Do you live your life as a Child of the Light?

It's true that we live in a world where there is undeniable darkness. Fear, violence, ignorance, hatred, closed-mindedness, and selfishness are an unfortunate part of our everyday lives. The question is, in the midst of this, can we still dedicate ourselves to live as Children of God and model a different way? Do our lives show a willingness to offer kindness, care, concern, open-mindedness, and respect for other people? Can we demonstrate trust in each other and in God's unfailing goodness? The letter to the Romans offers these words of advice for living out our Christianity:

> Let love be genuine; hate what is evil, hold fast to what is good; love one another with mutual affection; outdo one another in showing honor. Do not lag in zeal, be ardent in spirit, serve the Lord. Rejoice in hope, be patient in suffering, persevere in prayer. Contribute to the needs of the saints; extend hospitality to strangers. Bless those who persecute you; bless and do not curse them. Rejoice with those who rejoice, weep with those who weep. Live in harmony with one another; do not be haughty, but associate with the lowly, do not claim to be wiser than you are. Do not repay anyone evil for evil, but take thought for what is noble in the sight of all. If it is possible, so far as it depends on you, live peaceably with all. (Rom 12:9–18)

If we take our baptismal promises seriously, we are called to live in ways that testify to the transformational work God is doing in our lives. It is not enough to just know the words of God if they don't change the way we live. We have to "be doers of the word, and not merely hearers" (Jas 1:22). We are the ones who reflect God's presence in the world—we have the opportunity to be the hands, the feet, the voice, the touch, the very presence of God to other people. If we are going to live fully into our Christian beliefs, we must deliberately engage the complex issues that damage people, destroy families, and divide communities. We must speak out on issues of justice and peace, and we must pass these traits on to our godchildren.

When you read Scripture or discuss Christian behavior with your godchild, you are helping her understand what life in God's loving kingdom is all about. Your baptism has identified both of you as part of God's kingdom, and now you are ready to take action as official members of God's team. Being a Christian is not a passive endeavor. The prophet Micah told us to love kindness, but to *do* justice—our thoughts about faith need to be balanced with action. Standing up for God's ways, striving for true justice and lasting peace among all people are important. We can help live out these principles in our family life, at school, on the playground, in the workplace, and in our churches and communities. Look for opportunities to talk about how God's peace "surpasses all understanding" (Phil 4:7) and how God's justice may go beyond society's concept of simply what is fair or legal to show further dimensions of God's mercy.

Tracey's Story: Practicing Peace

We live in a busy, noisy, and sometimes scary world, a world where violence dominates our evening news, where traffic jams are commonplace, and where ongoing stress is part of everyone's life. Finding peace in the midst of this world can be very difficult.

When I became an Episcopalian almost seventeen years ago, one of the things I enjoyed most about my new tradition was "Passing the Peace" in church, a phrase that conjured up vivid images of transmitting God's peace from hand to hand, inviting it to gently rest on each person. As the world has become more and more unpredictable, the idea of passing God's peace along to other people has become even more meaningful to me.

On September 11, 2001, I was working at All Saints' Episcopal Church in downtown Atlanta. Our staff was gathered together for what was supposed to have been a full day of calendar planning. The events of that day changed all our plans. People were uncertain of what might happen next, and they were afraid to remain in tall city skyscrapers anywhere. Everyone just wanted to go home and be with the people they loved. Much of downtown was evacuated, but our priests chose to keep the church open for prayer. Many staff members went home, but several of us stayed to talk with people who came by or to work on creating a service where people could gather. From my office I watched people rush down the sidewalk. Cars inched their way to the crowded interstate, and frazzled people lined up at the subway station. It was all very surreal and very scary. I found myself wishing I could do something for them, wishing I could do something for myself to calm my racing mind and soothe my aching spirit. I wanted to do something, so I sat down at my computer and tried to write some suggestions for how parents could talk with their children about tragedy.

Offering concrete help to others was my first step to regaining balance, but it wasn't until later that I found something that helped me quiet some of my internal noise. Our church was filled to capacity with people looking for a solid place to stand. When we got to the passing of the peace, I was suddenly struck by how newly meaningful this ritual really was. Instead of just saying "peace" and quickly squeezing someone's hand as I usually did, I really looked into the tear-filled eyes of people around me, hugged them tight, and whispered, "God's Peace to you." I hadn't planned it—the words came from somewhere deep inside, from a place where I was hurting and wanting to feel better, from a place where the tangled details of my faith must live.

In the weeks, months, and now years that have ensued since that dreadful day, I have continued to look for ways to cultivate and practice the peace of God in my life. I attended numerous candlelight vigils. I signed petitions. I baked cookies and donated books to soldiers who are much too far from home. I accepted the fact that I am, at heart, a pacifist, and I have argued with people I love about the nature of war and whether or not human beings will ever find a better way to settle their differences. I read a lot of Anne Lamott and Frederick Buechner, who often give voice to the words in my head. I reconnected with old friends and tried to truly cherish the relationships in my life. I found a "Red Tent" full of women who helped me delve more deeply into

Scripture and gave me space and support to wrestle with my faith questions. I made more room in my life for quiet and meditation. I began signing all my letters "God's Peace to you" or the shortened version, "God's Peace."

None of these things are all that significant in the grand scheme of our busy, noisy world. But they are the things that help calm my heart and remind me that God's peace surpasses our understanding. They are my attempt to live out my ongoing prayer: "Let there be peace on earth and let it begin with me. . . ."

≶ Speak Your Mind Even if Your Voice Shakes

Our mandate to strive for justice and peace is clear. The Bible gives us instructions such as "Speak out for those who cannot speak, for the rights of all the destitute . . . defend the rights of the poor and needy" (Prov 31:8–9). We have the example of a God who cares for the poor and oppressed. Jesus himself also consistently reached out to people with little power or social standing: women, Samaritans, children, lepers, prostitutes, and poor people. Likewise we are called to speak for those who have no voice, but when we follow Jesus' example, we also need to be prepared to face the consequences for speaking out.

Jesus openly criticized some of the laws and policies of his day and even broke those laws when he felt they got in the way of what God was calling him to do. Speaking

Finding God's Justice and Peace

≈ Help your godchild understand what God's justice means, and talk about the places in your environment where you see injustice. How can you help?

≈ Make a prayer list together of places or people who need justice or peace. Make a copy for each of you and use your lists at mealtime or bedtime to remember a few names each day.

≈ As your godchild gets older, read the story of Jesus healing a man on the Sabbath in Matthew 12. Talk about why Jesus broke the law and what that might mean for us.

≈ Research together the life of someone who stood up for justice or peace. It can be someone famous like Mahatma Ghandi, Martin Luther King Jr., Rosa Parks, Mother Teresa, or Jimmy Carter, but it might also be someone from your own life, or even you!

≈ Study local and national government policies with your godchild. Remind her that living in a community gives us the responsibility to use the power of our citizenship to promote justice. Many people believe that you can define a nation or an individual person by the way they treat the weakest and most vulnerable among them.

Finding God's Justice and Peace (continued)

≷ Search the Scriptures for examples and instructions about working for justice and peace. Use a concordance to search for words like justice, peace, orphan, or oppressed. Write down special verses or phrases such as "let justice roll down like waters" (Amos 5:24).

≷ Read stories or watch movies that depict people standing up for what is right. Talk about how you might react in a similar situation.

≷ Talk about war and what it costs emotionally, spiritually, and financially. Brainstorm alternative ways to resolve conflict and talk about how we can be active peacemakers.

≷ Find ways to remember, thank, support, and pray for the people whose job it is to help fight for justice or keep the peace—police officers, soldiers, lawyers, judges, lawmakers, to name a few. Who else can you think of?

≷ Think about what it means to be a peacemaker. Is it the same thing as a peacekeeper? How are the two similar and how are they different?

≷ Light a candle with your godchild. Remember that we are called to be Children of Light—shining a candle of God's love into the dark places of the world. Pray for peace in our homes, in our lives, and in our world.

out for justice or peace sometimes means saying things that are unpopular or will make people angry. We are often afraid of those who appear stronger than us, but when we partner with God, we enter into life in God's kingdom and recognize that we are under God's ultimate authority. This gives us strength to be merciful and gracious even to those who previously, in our fear, we may have thought were stronger than us. When we immerse ourselves in God's love and give voice to what we know is right, we may find ourselves to be stronger than we ever dreamed, because we are allied with God.

It is sometimes scary to speak out—whether it is standing up to a playground bully or voicing an unpopular opinion about ethics in the workplace—but it is important to talk with your godchild about ways you both can do this in your everyday lives. Maggie Kuhn, a great social activist who fought against age discrimination, offers this wonderful piece of advice: "Speak your mind, even if your voice shakes." As Christians, we have the backing of a God who gives us strength and courage to do the work that needs to be done.

Living according to God's Rules

When we read about the early church in the book of Acts, we see a great passion for justice and peace. The early followers were eager to share their possessions with one another and to share with others the good news of

God in Christ (Acts 2:42–47). They had extraordinary enthusiasm and spirit. This description of the church community comes just after the story of the Holy Spirit arriving on the day of Pentecost, and the two things seem intrinsically linked. When we partner with God, we are filled with the Holy Spirit and energized to do God's work. We are on fire and have a devotion to the task that is all-consuming. This is what it means to be baptized with both water and the Spirit. In the baptism ceremony, your godchild's candle is lit from the fire of the Christ candle and then entrusted to you. As a godparent, you must be careful to always protect that flame, being mindful not to quench the Spirit that may be manifested in your young godchild in surprising ways.

One of the ways to help your godchild understand the need for justice and peace is by simply teaching her the basic rules of living in God's kingdom. The same way you would explain to a young child the rules for visiting at your home or being in church or school, you can explain some of God's rules. A good place to start is with the summary of the law that Jesus offers: "'You shall love the Lord your God with all your heart, with all your soul, and with all your mind.' This is the greatest and first commandment. And a second is like it: 'You shall love your neighbor as yourself'" (Matt 22:37–39). You may also want to read the Ten Commandments with your godchild (see below) or act out the Scripture passages and compare them to other life situations.

When you begin to understand how God's kingdom reflects God's presence, you can identify ways in which we need to work to bring our world into closer alignment with God's ideals. As you talk with your godchild about the principles of God's kingdom, look for ways you can both get involved. Is there a specific injustice you want to follow in the news and pray about? Do you see a cause you want to support by writing letters or volunteering? Is there a special project you and your godchild can take on together?

⸗ Shaping Our Lives: The Ten Commandments

The Ten Commandments give us something we can shape our lives around. The original Ten Commandments appear twice in the Hebrew Scriptures—Exodus 20:2–17 and Deuteronomy 5:6-21—but they appear as part of the catechism in our Episcopal Book of Common Prayer in the slightly altered (and enlightening) form seen below. The original wording of the Ten Commandments can also be found in our prayer book on pages 317–18 and a shorter, more modern version on page 350.

Q. What is our duty to God?

A. Our duty is to believe and trust in God;

    I To love and obey God and to bring others to know him;

    II To put nothing in the place of God;

III To show God respect in thought, word, and deed;

IV And to set aside regular times for worship, prayer, and the study of God's ways.

Q. What is our duty to our neighbors?

A. Our duty to our neighbors is to love them as ourselves, and to do to other people as we wish them to do to us;

V To love, honor, and help our parents and family; to honor those in authority, and to meet their just demands;

VI To show respect for the life God has given us; to work and pray for peace; to bear no malice, preju dice, or hatred in our hearts; and to be kind to all the creatures of God;

VII To use all our bodily desires as God intended;

VIII To be honest and fair in our dealings; to seek justice, freedom, and the necessities of life for all people; and to use our talents and possessions as ones who must answer for them to God;

IX To speak the truth, and not to mislead others by our silence;

X To resist temptations to envy, greed, and jealousy; to rejoice in other people's gifts and graces; and to do our duty for the love of God, who has called us into fellowship with him. (BCP, 847–48)

⚡ The Power of Fire

On the day of Pentecost, the Holy Spirit came rushing into the upper room where the disciples were gathered together, and tongues of fire were said to have appeared above each of their heads. This was the birthday, or better yet, the baptism day of the church. But this story can sometimes make the coming of God's Spirit seem like something just for special holy people in a faraway time and place. In fact, the coming of the Holy Spirit is meant for all baptized Christians—including both you and your godchild. The fire that appeared on that first Christian Pentecost is one of the Spirit's symbols of power. In the baptism ceremony we remember this fire when the Easter candle lights the baptismal candle of our newest member. The baptismal candle is then passed to the parents or godparents. All are now "on fire"—and called to action in the Lord's service.

Think about all the qualities of fire: it warms, enlightens, purifies, clarifies, and it can even change the nature of elements it touches. The fire we are given at baptism helps empower us to do God's work in the world. You may wish to use a candle-lighting ceremony with your godchild to remind you both of the Holy Spirit's power within you. You can do this anytime, but the yearly anniversary of your godchild's baptism is a great time to relight her baptismal candle, review the ceremony, and renew the covenant established by God and accepted by you both in ever-deepening ways. Light your godchild's baptismal candle (or a special one you keep for this purpose) and as you do, read, and discuss the baptism liturgy (BCP, 299–311). Renewing your baptismal covenant with God is an excellent activity to celebrate your godchild's "baptism birthday."

God's Words about Fire

Burning bush	Exodus 3:1–6
Israelites led by pillar of fire	Exodus 13:17–22
Offering made through fire	Exodus 30:20
God as consuming fire	Deuteronomy 4:23–24; Hebrews 12:28–29
Chariot of fire to heaven	2 Kings 2:9–12
Three men survive in fiery furnace	Daniel 3:1–30
Jesus will baptize with fire	Matthew 3:11–12
Let your light shine	Matthew 5:14–16
Flames appear on Pentecost	Acts 2:1–4

Chapter 8

"I Can Do It Myself!"

Renewing the Covenant
Made at Baptism

"Open their hearts to your grace and truth. Fill
them with your holy and life-giving Spirit. Keep them
in the faith and communion of your holy Church.
Teach them to love others. . . ."

The concluding chapter of this book, like so many chapters in our lives, is not really an ending but rather an invitation to all that comes next. We have journeyed through the questions of our baptismal covenant, but there is still a lifetime of loving and learning ahead for you and your godchild. This last chapter is like a compass, a small treasure to tuck in your pocket that is meant to help you keep your bearings and find your way. It offers just a few short words to see you through some major transitions, much like the way the Gospels encapsulate all of Jesus' adolescence and young adulthood in these brief words: "Jesus increased in wisdom and in years, and in divine and human favor" (Luke 2:52).

When you first become a godparent, the responsibility to represent both God and the gathered community of faith may seem overwhelming. But the years go by so quickly and God truly does work in mysterious and miraculous ways. As this child grows and matures and God is revealed to him more and more, we pray he will someday decide to take on for himself the vows made for him at baptism. At some point, we all have to make a personal decision about following Christ, and answer the same question Jesus asked his disciples so long ago: "But who do you say that I am?" (Matt 16:13–20). When your godchild can answer as Peter did, "You are the Messiah, the Son of the living God," he is ready to make a public profession of his faith. In many denominations this decision is marked with the ceremony, or sacrament, of confirmation—the day you publicly and personally confirm and embrace the covenant made on the day of baptism.

⋛ Independent Does Not Mean Alone

Like a parent leaving on a trip, there are so many things we, as godparents, will want to tell our young people as they embark on their own journey. We want to remind them of all we've tried to teach them and all we hope they have absorbed, and so we are tempted to call out words of wisdom as they go forth: "Remember that God loves you and so do I. Remember that you have been bought with a price (1 Cor 6:20) and that your life is of inestimable value—don't waste it. Remember that it's okay to make mistakes, but there is no mistake you can make, no path you can *ever* find yourself on that could take you outside the realm of God's attention and concern. Remember to go to church; you need other people. Don't be afraid to ask big questions—God can handle it. Watch for God's presence in the world, and you'll be astonished by how often you find it. Make the most of the gifts you have been given. Remember what's important, let go of what's not. Remember that you are dust and to dust you shall return, but in the meantime, walk as a Child of the Light, and remember that God's words live in you."

And as your godchild takes the first tentative steps in his own journey, he will probably be most excited and motivated by the prospect of independence. Becoming independent is important, but godparents can help older godchildren see that even when we are independent, we are still interdependent with other people. As independent people, we become aware of our own unique gifts and abilities, and we learn skills that help us become competent, self-reliant people. But even then, we still need connections with other people because we live as part of an interdependent society. And as we learn in early childhood, there really is safety in numbers, and it really is easier and more effective to be a member of a team—as reflected in both the concepts of "Body of Christ" and "Kingdom of God."

There is a whole planet full of people that God has given to each other. There are many ways we can experience being part of God's loving family. Perhaps we find this in the families we are born into, or perhaps as we get older, we find ways to extend or create families that meet those needs. The godparent/godchild relationship may be one such extension of God's family, and even beyond the god-family, there is a larger church family who commit to support their fellow Christians when asked, "Will you who witness these vows do all in your power to support these persons in their life in Christ?" (BCP, 303). Both the godparent and godchild can receive support and guidance through such a community.

Even more than our lives are connected with each other, they are also connected with God. As far back as the

Garden of Eden, there has been a struggle between independence and intimacy. When Adam and Eve first fell for the temptation to disregard God's ways, they broke the intimate relationship they had with God and hid away their true selves. We sometimes fall into this same pattern—we ignore God, turning away from God's love and forgetting our special covenantal relationship. But even then, the covenant is not broken. Jesus offers a way to restore that relationship and like the father in the Prodigal Son story, God is merciful and stands waiting with open arms for us to "come to ourselves" and return (Luke 15:11–32).

Speaking the Truth in Love

As we learn to make choices, it is inevitable that sometimes we will make wrong choices. When we make mistakes, we have to learn how to name what is happening, take responsibility for our choices, and then look for ways to change our course. As a godparent, you are accountable to the sacred promises you made to God, and so your job is not just to be some kindly adult who brings presents and shares happy things about God. Be quick to praise your godchild, but be honest when you see behavior that is less than praiseworthy. If you see bad habits or destructive patterns developing, part of your responsibility is to have an honest conversation with your godchild about what you see and what your concerns are. It can be uncomfortable to have conversations like this, but speaking the truth in love to your godchild will help him learn to do the same. When he sees a community that is not functioning well, he will have an idea of how to speak out in appropriate, considerate ways.

LaTisha's Story: My Maturing Godson

My godchild turned eighteen last year. Legally he is an adult, but at times he still needs guidance, support, and Christian advice. One night a few months ago, he called to tell me about a road trip he was planning. He was excited about visiting another state to see his girlfriend.

"Wow," I said, "what does your dad think about that?" After listening to my godson's reply, it became apparent that the conversation with his father had shut down after Dad's initial response of "That's not a good idea." My godchild was frustrated that his dad didn't seem to want him to grow up. He still intended to make the trip and was calling me for support. He seemed determined to make an independent decision, but he also wanted approval and direction from a trusted adult.

This is one of those times when godparents need the Holy Spirit's calm guidance. (Ask and you shall receive, seek and you shall find [Luke 11:9]) I took a deep breath and said, "Sweetie, you're still going to have to talk to your dad about your decision, you know. Maybe he would feel better about this if he knew you'd thought it all out. Have you let Tiffany's folks know that you'll be in town? What will you and Tiffany be doing together when you're there? Where are you going to stay? What will you do if things don't go right? Are you sure this is what you want to do?"

I tried to ask open, nonjudgmental questions and listen calmly and objectively to his answers. I tried to talk with him as an adult and encourage him to use his most mature decision-making skills. I did not try to convince him one way or the other, but I hope I helped him look at the consequences for whichever decision he made. After all, isn't that what a godparent is for?

When you face difficult situations and are seeking strength, you may find the words from the prayer at the end of the baptism ceremony to be especially helpful:

Deliver them, O Lord, from the way of sin and death.
Open their hearts to your grace and truth.
Fill them with your holy and life-giving Spirit.
Keep them in the faith and communion of your
    holy Church.
Teach them to love others in the power of the Spirit.
Send them into the world in witness to your love.
Bring them to the fullness of your peace and glory.

(See BCP, 305–6)

⩓ A Compass Tool: The Book of Common Prayer

When our spiritual life takes a detour, we may need some help to find our way back home. One of the best ways to do this is to pray, and a great tool for learning about prayer is the Book of Common Prayer. You may wish to have your own BCP at home, and you might consider giving this as a special gift to your godchild when they are old enough to use it. Even if you are not an Episcopalian, you may find this book a great addition to the books or prayers of your own tradition. The BCP is a rich source of ritual, prayer, and meditation. Explore the pages and you will find many resources for personal and family devotional time. Some highlights include:

- ⩓ Morning, noon, evening, and nighttime prayer activities (pp. 37–127)
- ⩓ Daily devotions for individuals and families (pp. 136–46)
- ⩓ Prayers for various seasons and occasions throughout the church year
- ⩓ Liturgies for Lent and Easter (pp. 264–95)
- ⩓ Sacramental celebrations such as baptism, Eucharist, confirmation, and marriage
- ⩓ Ordination services (pp. 510ff.)
- ⩓ The Psalms (pp. 585ff.)
- ⩓ Prayers and thanksgivings—dozens of them (pp. 810ff.)

- ☙ An outline of the faith, or catechism (pp. 845ff.)
- ☙ Historical documents of the Episcopal Church (pp. 864ff.)

☙ The Church Year

As your godchild grows, he will become more familiar with the rhythm of our church year. The liturgical calendar is one of the great gifts of our Christian tradition. Year after year, we follow the same pattern and hear the same Scriptures or lessons, and over time, we are shaped by this rhythm and repetition. Even when we encounter the same words year after year, they are new each time we hear them because *we* are new each time we hear them. Our perspective on faith, and our interaction with it, is always changing because our relationship with God is always changing and growing and deepening. As you and your godchild experience the different seasons and sacraments, here are some activities you can share together:

Enjoying the Rhythm of the Seasons

Advent

- ☙ Our church year begins with Advent. Share an Advent calendar that highlights the religious significance of waiting and preparing for the Christ Child (not one that just focuses on gifts or candy).

Enjoying the Rhythm
of the Seasons (continued)

≋ Many churches offer Advent Wreath Making work-
shops, but even if your church doesn't, you may want
to make a wreath with your godchild.

≋ Research prayers or readings to use with your Advent
wreath—suggestions to get you started can be found
at www.godparenting.info.

≋ Write your own prayer service to include the concerns and hopes of family, community, and world.

Christmas

≋ Volunteer to spend a day with your godchild so
parents can do extra Christmas shopping or errands.

≋ Join or organize a caroling trip to a local nursing
home or hospital. Even children who can't read yet
usually know (or can learn) some Christmas carols
and will enjoy the trip.

≋ Adopt a special service project during the holiday
season—write cards to people who might be lonely,
be a Secret Santa, or volunteer at a soup kitchen or
other organization.

≋ There are many special holiday services—choose one
or more to attend with your godchild.

Enjoying the Rhythm
of the Seasons (continued)

Epiphany

- ⅔ Celebrate the gift of light by giving a special flashlight, nightlight, or candle.

- ⅔ Look at the stars with your godchild and read the story of the Magi's journey to the Christ Child (Matt 2:1–12).

- ⅔ Give gifts to others and honor the gifts God has given you.

Lent

- ⅔ Make a Lenten calendar with suggestions of small sacrifices or good deeds each day, such as write a letter of encouragement, help someone with a project, say a special prayer.

- ⅔ Walk a Stations of the Cross. Look at the pictures, talk about the story. Encourage your godchild to ask questions and think about what each station means.

- ⅔ Share or discuss some of the special Holy Week services before Easter.

- ⅔ If your church offers foot washing on Maundy Thursday, consider sharing this special symbol of servant leadership with your godchild.

Enjoying the Rhythm
of the Seasons (continued)

Easter

≋ In the Great Vigil of Easter, even young children can appreciate the symbols of light, music, and alleluias. Make it a tradition to attend this service with your godchild.

≋ Visit your godchild's family on, or near, Easter Sunday and share a meal together.

Pentecost

≋ Use Pentecost to remind your godchild about the gifts of the Holy Spirit that all Christians share—the gifts of hope, power, and comfort.

≋ As your godchild gets older, help him identify his particular spiritual gifts (1 Cor 12:1–12).

≋ Create a Pentecost Play Day during which you play with wind toys such as kites or bubbles. You might also make candles or eat cinnamon "red hots" to remember fire. Wear red since it is the color of Pentecost.

≋ Choose an activity where both you and your godchild can be "on fire" in loving service to God.

⧖ Holidays and Holy Days

There are many special days of celebration in our lives, and you can help your godchild understand that while holy days like Christmas and Easter are natural times to talk about God, *any* celebration can be a reminder that God is present in our world. In her novel *Walking on Water*, Madeleine L'Engle writes, "There is nothing so secular that it cannot be sacred and that is one of the deepest messages of the Incarnation." When we believe that God became incarnate and took on human form, we also realize that almost any tradition or custom that celebrates life and rebirth can help us focus our thoughts on the God who always celebrates life. For instance, swim parties can remind us of the water used in baptism, and birthday parties can help us celebrate another year of our life with Christ as we enjoy being with friends and family.

⧖ Special Days for Baptism

There are four days during the church year when baptism is most appropriate for accepting new members into the Christian community: The Easter Vigil, the Day of Pentecost, All Saints Day (or the Sunday following), and the Feast of the Baptism of Jesus. In fact, if there are no baptisms scheduled, the Book of Common Prayer suggests that the congregation's Renewal of Baptismal Vows take the place of the Nicene Creed on these feast days, as it does during the service of Holy Baptism (p. 312).

Each of these occasions is a great time to help your godchild see the connection between his own story and the larger story of the Christian church. When we remember Jesus' baptism, we also can pledge ourselves again to follow Christ's example. When we celebrate All Saints Day, we commemorate all baptized persons—those living and those who have gone before us—and we remember that each saint has a story to tell. The Day of Pentecost will help your godchild appreciate the tremendous strength and power of the Holy Spirit, and remind him that he too has been baptized by water and the fire of God's Spirit. And the Great Vigil of Easter is an especially moving service that is full of mystery and symbolism.

The Easter Vigil is the first service of Easter—it happens somewhere between sunset on Holy Saturday and sunrise on Easter Sunday. In the early church, it was often the preferred occasion for baptizing new converts. The Vigil begins with The Service of Light, where a "new" fire (often started with flint and steel) is kindled in the darkness. The Paschal (or Easter) Candle is lit from the new fire and then used to light the participants' candles. Those gathered process into the church bearing the Light of Christ. This powerful service moves us from the darkness of night to the light of Easter morning and helps us more fully grasp the emotions and reality of Jesus' life, death, and resurrection.

Why Wait?

Darkness (sin . . . death . . . fear)
Brightness!?
New fire from flint (ancient . . . primordial)
"The Light of Christ!"
 resurrection
 life
 wonder and *awe*!
Fire spread and shared
Procession (leading . . . following . . . journeying . . .)
 Following the candle
 following Christ
 following the light
 walking with fellow Christians
 walking in the footsteps of Jesus (dead? but *risen*?)
 following Christ to new life!
 "This is the night!"
 of Christ's *victory*!
Stories—many, many stories
 (and psalms and prayers and songs)
 Creation
 Flood
 Exodus
 New heart = new spirit
 God's holy people
 History lessons
 ancient history

our history
salvation history!
Renew, *relive*, covenant with God . . .
proposal and agreement
protection and commitment
devotion and partnership

Baptism
"Do You Believe?"
water
fire
oil
all salvation history
our baptismal salvation
Jesus' death
our death
Jesus' life
our new life
Communion

(poem by Nancy Ann McLaughlin)

As you and your godchild journey throughout the seasons of your life, we pray you both will always know that wherever you are, you rest in the palm of God's loving hand. May we all continue to grow in grace and knowledge, and may we be forever enriched by any relationship in which we experience true God-parenting.